Lorne Foreshore, September 1953

You might not know where you're going ...

First published by Busybird Publishing 2019

Copyright © 2019 Martin Fowler

ISBN 978-1-925949-95-7

Martin Fowler has asserted his right under the Copyright, Designs and Patents Act 1988 to be identified as the author of this work. The information in this book is based on the author's experiences and opinions. The publisher specifically disclaims responsibility for any adverse consequences, which may result from use of the information contained herein. Permission to use information has been sought by the author. Any breaches will be rectified in further editions of the book.

All rights reserved. No part of this publication may be reproduced, stored in or introduced into a retrieval system, or transmitted in any form, or by any means (electronic, mechanical, photocopying, recording or otherwise) without the prior written permission of the author. Any person who does any unauthorised act in relation to this publication may be liable to criminal prosecution and civil claims for damages. Enquiries should be made through the publisher.

Cover image: Kev Howlett
Cover design: Busybird Publishing
Layout and typesetting: Busybird Publishing

Busybird Publishing
2/118 Para Road
Montmorency, Victoria
Australia 3094
www.busybird.com.au

Lines of the Times

A Travel Scrapbook – The Journal Notes of Martin Fowler

1973–2016

Martin Fowler

To Jack and Betty, in memory.

Andy and Lis.

Preface

The author was born in Melbourne, 1950 and has travelled both painfully and well in Asia and around the globe for 40 years.

Enjoys surfing, his friends, food and wine, as well as sitting around with music and books in his beach apartment in Lorne.

Never let school interfere with his education and regularly works to support his travel habits. Has partnered both a bungalow and a canoe in Bali with KG, as well as a Porsche and Rolls Royce with S.B. and N.L.

Served briefly as cellarmaster on the ketch 'Sailmaker IV'. Once waitered on the Italian Ambassador in Hanoi, kayaked in France with G.V. on the Gulfe du Morbihan, volcano trekked in Indonesia with T.M., hiked NZ with A.F. and T.A., boated on the Mekong, cycled down Broadway with The Russo, walked until five am across the breadth of Paris with The Tiger, shared numerous G & T's with A & P, K & G in our respective Bali homes.

These writings are for all of you – to a fine family and to a fine group of friends at home and abroad.

Thank you, love you all.

Long may you run.

MF
2018

'Travelling is Victory.'
>An old Arab proverb, from when travellers were once a mobile elite.

You have to do something at 35,000 ft for long hours. These journal entries, notes, extracts and observations have been compiled over eight round-world air tickets, and thirty plus visits to Indonesia and South East Asia. France and the USA both kicked in as major sponsors from July 1997. It's an A–Z of how I've travelled, with observations of some of the cultural habits and recondite rituals of the world I've grown up on.

Life is long; it really is very fantastic and I have found it amusing rather than a serious business, even after a life-stopping heart attack in 2012. For 90% of my life I've been fortunate to travel, the other 10% has been a little wasted. Where possible I have acknowledged the writers and sources of the bits and pieces, but some plagiarism may have crept in along the way. If it sounded or looked good, I wrote it down. If I have failed to acknowledge you, sorry.

'*Nothing, of course, begins at the time you think it did.*'

Writer, Lillian Hellman.

Hawaii, 2016

A

as in Ageing

(But you are just the same age as you've always been.)

*'You can't reach old age
by another man's road.
My habits protect my life
but they would
assassinate you.'*
        Part of Mark Twain's 70th Birthday speech.

*D*on't you love the way life has been designed. You just get your head together and then your body starts falling apart. But as the author A. Punch McGregor suggested, 'it's all about amore-fate; you have to be in love with your fate.'

The secret is to try and stay ahead in the race against getting older. To start regretting the things you did and not the things you didn't do. Now that your back is going out more than you are, and that you are looking at the menu more than the waitress, it's your travels that can help make a life longer and richer.

It was Camus who wrote 'Make haste to enjoy yourself, gather your happiness quickly, for in its shadow pain and death grow side by side.'

Bali journal, 2001

'I think perhaps that growing old and slightly dippy at the same time might not be entirely awful: not being in full possession of the ball must provide a sort of local anaesthetic to dull the realization that the game will soon be over.'

> Jane Fraser
> *The Australian*, 10/92

'60 isn't old; if you're a tree.'

Unknown

'Swim, dance a little, go to Paris every August and live within walking distance of two hospitals.'

> Horse trainer,
> Horatio Luro
> explaining the secret
> of his eighty years.

The muddle that men get into around the time of midlife can be traced back to their diminishing drive to reproduce... towards middle age men's biology begins winding down. Although they still desire intercourse, it no longer preoccupies them in the same way. As this desire lessens, so do all the social behaviours that go with it.

As part of their reproductive display, younger men are careful about their image. They watch what they say and do, don't admit weakness and want to appear dominant and successful. Biologically they are hardwired to preserve their genes and to do this they have to get as many women as possible to swim in their gene pool...

... The male body has a good 20 or 30 years to reproduce its genes and after that, biochemical changes make it much less interested in doing so...

Although initially there is much denial about age-related changes, the psychological shifts of midlife result from this winding down. In an often-unconscious way, reflection on this leads to behavioural changes...

... Some of the changes men feel in midlife are similar to the changes they experienced in adolescence. Teenagers are in turmoil because they are logging into the big reproductive phase of their lives. The hard and aggressive race to reproduction is beginning.

They feel confused, and responses to ordinary events are inconsistent. 'What's it all about?' they ask.

"As middle-aged men log out of this program, they too want to know what it's all about.'
    Extract found in article by Jill Margo
    'Get A Rise Out of Middle Age'
    1992 (published in The Australian)

Reporter: 'What do you expect the future to be like?'
Old woman: 'Very short.'
> (one of the oldest women in France, spoken during birthday interview.)

' *Age only matters when one is ageing. Now that I have arrived at a great age, I might just as well be twenty.*' '
>   Pablo Picasso

'*Learn from the mistakes of others. You can't live long enough to make them all yourself.*'
Eleanor Roosevelt

'*How old would you be if you didn't know how old you are?*'
Satchel Paige

'*Old age and treachery will always overcome youth and enthusiasm*'
David Mamet,
Sydney–Hobart race
contestant, 2008

'*It's high time for me to depart, for at my age I now begin to see things as they really are.*'

> Philosopher, Le Bovier De Fontenelle

'*Never have I enjoyed youth so thoroughly as I have in my old age.*'

> Writer, George Santayana

'*And a woman of 90 said to de Fontenelle, then 95; 'Death has forgotten us.'*

'Shh', said de Fontenelle, putting his finger to his lips.'

> France Journal, 2002

'*Guilt shows clearest on the faces of older people, whose skin is so full of detail*'

> Writers, P. Theroux

B

as in Books & Writing

(or to never ask in a bookstore where the self-help section is.)

*M*any *people are afraid of emptiness, because it reminds them of loneliness. Everything has to be filled in, it seems – appointment books, hillsides, vacant lots – but when all the spaces are filled, the loneliness really begins. Then the groups are joined, the classes are signed up for, and the Gift-to-yourself items are bought. When the loneliness starts creeping in the door, the television sets are turned on to make it go away. But it doesn't go away. So some of us do instead, and after discarding the emptiness of the Big Congested Mess, we discover the fullness of nothing...*

from The Tao of Pooh

By Benjamin Hoff

〜〜
〜〜

As Lord Henry said to Dorian Gray, 'The true mystery of the world is the visible ... it is only the shallow people who do not judge by appearances.'

〜〜
〜〜

My childhood home and Justus Jorgensen's art colony were only a few miles from each other. Yet they might have been centuries or planets apart. Where our house was a triple fronted weatherboard that sat squarely on its standard 60 feet block, Seb's was a gargoyle Elizabethan hall surrounded by a sprawling collection of Brueghel – like cottages that dominated the district's most impressive hill. Jorgie's chip on Eltham's shoulder ...

Where we had a Ford Consul in our garage. Jorgie had an ark in his, a vast and old barge that he laboured on like some latter day Noah, behind giant, cathedral-style doors acquired from the burnt-out shell of Melbourne University's Wilson Hall. Apparently Jorgie intended to live his final day within that ancient hull, though most of us saw it as his funeral barque ...

Certainly Jorgensen's Eltham became something of an outer-suburban Montmartre or Greenwich Village. Much writing, theatre and film making owes some small debt to his influence or at least to his example. Meanwhile the wider community visits Montsalvat as if it were some Disneyland, but some of the values built into those beautiful buildings must rub off...

It might seem that Australia was the last country on earth where you'd expect to find a Jorgensen. But I've a contrary theory that goes something like this: because of our society's crassness, because of our lack of history, of European richness, because of the boredom produced by our remoteness and, for many years, our oppressive censorship, social tensions were created that produced a number of extraordinary paradoxical figures...

I'd like to pay tribute to Jorgensen. And I hope that the memory of this magnificent ratbag lives on in Montsalvat, not so much as an inspiration to others but as a mystery, as a nagging doubt, a constant questioning of glib, comfortable assumptions.

    extract from Phillip Adams column in The Age, May 1975[1]

---

1. Included as a homage to the art colony at Monsalvat, where I'd visit to muck around after school with classmate Marcus Skipper in the late '50's. Always a place of intrigue, it was walking distance from my State School and bike distance from home

Such a vast country; it cannot possibly function properly over those distances. Alcohol laws draconian and different depending in which Province. Quebec makes move to secede from the rest and vigorously retaining its French history and mannerisms. To be bagels or baguettes?

5071 kms from Montreal to Quebec, Toronto, Thunder Bay, Winnipeg, Regina, Calgary, Banff, Lake Louise and finally to Vancouver – moose in the wild, tee pees and reservations. Met my first red indian. Said the Government had just allocated them another 1000 square miles of reservation. 'What do we want with another area of rock and dirt?'

No mobile phone invasion – generally looked on as bad manners in public. No 'personal' number plates on cars. They were called 'Vanity Plates' in Quebec and considered not appropriate. And Niagara Falls – all that beauty spoilt with the surrounding kiosks, paved concrete and roadway next to it. 'Niagfa' Falls seemed a more appropriate name.

Canada journal
July 1987

Departures. They were always the same. Always the first departures over the sea. People have always left the land in the same sorrow and despair, but that never stopped men from going, Jews, philosophers and pure travellers for the journey's own sake. Nor did it ever stop women letting them go, the women who never went themselves, who stayed behind to look after the birthplace, the race, the property, the reason for the return. For centuries, because of the ships, journeys were longer and more tragic than they are today. A voyage covered its distance in a natural span of time. People were used to those slow human speeds on both land and sea, to those delays, those waiting on the wind or fair weather, to those expectations of shipwreck, sun and death.

>   Found in The Lover, Marguerite Duras 1984

Vietnam Journal
August 1995

〰〰

*A*h, to be enjoying the beauty of 2 summers in the one year again.

But why does it get increasingly difficult to do this? Trying to plot the right travel route and airfare, packing suitable clothes and at the same time getting into the right mood for the next month or so.

And so with the books that must go with you. The reading has to be in harmony with where you are located.

And books and reading are an important part of my travels – an escape from what the year has crowded out.

As Margo Jefferson wrote in the NY Times book review sometime this year, 'whatever your need, fulfil it, whatever your mood, indulge it.'

Paris journal
August 2002

... There is no evidence to suggest that those who read a lot are better than those who don't ... But does this mean... that books cannot teach us about life or how to live? It's true that we can't expect – and most of us surely, have no desire – to find neat moral lessons wrapped up in our favourite books. Good books are not didactic. Nevertheless, reading can have a profound, and profoundly humanising, effect on our lives. Literature has its own ways of teaching us about life and living.

The central experience in reading is of immersion, of entering so completely into the world of the story that everything else fades away. When this happens we are opening ourselves up to a very different way of knowing. Not just our minds and our consciousness but our whole self is brought into play.

We register impressions at all levels of being, conscious and unconscious, visceral and cerebral, instinctual and aesthetic. Our deepest prejudices and ideals are engaged, along with the detritus of language and culture that contributes to who we are.

... Through reading, we rehearse the great dilemmas of life, both personal and social. We find ourselves asking the philosophical questions: How should I live? What is the good life? What is love? What is justice? And what does it all add up to?

Literature is not philosophy, it's not psychology and it's certainly not religion or theology. But it is a form of knowledge that tells us about who we are, about ourselves, our society and our culture ... Reading enables us to reflect on elements of existence we don't encounter anywhere else, and to do it in a unique way. It enables us, in the words of Virginia Woolf, 'to learn through feeling' ... Literature does not give us a set of rules for living but it gives us a wider frame of reference, and it does enable us to reflect more broadly and engage more deeply.

... Does this make readers morally better people? Of course not. Yet there can be no doubt that reading has the potential to enrich our lives and make us more humane. In bringing us into contact with the inner lives of others – fictional characters as well as writers – reading makes it difficult to withhold our empathy in the real world...

    taken from article by Ann-Marie Priest

    Weekend Australian 20-01-07

THE GOD OF SMALL THINGS

'... The Great Stories are the ones you have heard and want to hear again. The ones you can enter anywhere and inhabit comfortably. They don't deceive you with thrills and trick endings. They don't surprise you with the unforeseen. They are as familiar as the house you live in. Or the smell of your lover's skin. You know how they end, yet you listen as though you don't. In the way that although you know that one day you will die, you live as though you won't. In the Great Stories you know who lives, who dies, who finds love, who doesn't. And yet you want to know again. That is their mystery and their magic ...'

    Extract reprinted by permission of Harper Collins Publishers Ltd © Arundhati Roy 2011

Bali, 2014

≈≈

'Let's tone down the wacky claims about national identity and embrace more complicated truths ...

Barbeques to start with. OK, I don't think the Russians barbeque much, but cooking meat over flames is reasonably common wherever humans gather ...

This notion that our irony is a defining national characteristic: forget it. Other cultures say the opposite of what they mean. And even in Australia, the use of irony and dry humour is not universal. I've met plenty of humourless Australians in my time ...

... Our unique love of sport is shared by only the other 190 or so nations that turn up at the Olympics. Or the football World Cup. Turn a corner anywhere in the world where there's decent reception, and there'll be a bunch of blokes huddled around a telly watching sport. Probably betting on it.

Oh, but we love a beer. So do the Belgians. And the Americans again. Over there you can buy it in the supermarkets ...

Letters are acts of faith; telephone calls are a reflex.

found in NY Times

August 1994

I heard a Yemeni blogger this week, when asked what had prompted their protests, say 'we just want the normal human rights'.

That's the world we're in. That's the world that's coming. Not a world where we all retreat to our patch and make some parochial claim for how unique it is; the national equivalent of those who refer to their suburb or town as 'God's own country'.

But a world where we expect everyone to have the same human rights. A world where we are all connected and can all hear and see what everyone else is doing. And in that world, our claims of our unique take on how we do things starts to look distinctly childish.

This is the real end of the constant search for Australian identity.

Let's take a good hard look at ourselves and see who we really are right now ...

The sooner we recognise ourselves as an immigrant nation and celebrate that, the closer we'll get to the truth of ourselves. And it wouldn't hurt us to acknowledge we're an immigrant nation that dispossessed and shattered our first Australians.

And the sooner we make 'I am Australian' our national anthem, the cheerier our national events will become.

It's a time of truth. It's a time when people so much worse off than ourselves are staking their lives on being a part of this great world. We don't have to take to the streets. But we could step forward and admit who we really are.'

    extract from article by James Valentine

    Weekend Australian, 19 FEBRUARY 2011

'... For the French protect their privacy with a sacred fury and prefer the permissiveness of sophisticated silence to the pleasure of spicy gossip (or 'crusty' as the French say – 'croustillant)'.

And the Paris bookstore, selling art books – Mona Lisait (Mona was reading).

Paris Journal, 2003.

~~~

And books and bookstores were to become obsolete, as digital print gradually consumed the market?

I don't think so. It was encouraging in Paris to see amidst the plethora of smart phones on buses and trains that people were still reading books. No headphones, no ear plugs, mobile phones neatly put away and pages being turned. Evidence that people are still thinking.

Made me remember, too, the comment by Jane Smiley, an American author, that many people like herself (and myself!) felt better at the mere sight of a book.

<div align="right">Paris journal, 2016</div>

~~~

Hey citizens! Have you ever thought about the enormous debt we all owe to the men and women of the advertising profession? After all, if not for their tireless efforts, how would we ever be able to choose the mass-produced consumer items best suited to our individual lifestyles?

    Tom Tomorrow (alias Dan Perkins)

    Political Cartoonist

    Paris 2002

It's a powerful thing to let ourselves consciously realise how brief even a long life actually is. Perhaps that's why motivational stories remain so popular. Often the central message they bring is that a brush with death or a hard-won recovery from a tragedy, has dramatically reminded the person how immeasurably precious life really is. Along with that shake-up, or course, comes the realisation that life is fragile, hazardous and unpredictable as well as marvellous, and that every day truly counts...

In the wake of a tragedy or a near miss, we may tell ourselves we will live differently and much more appreciatively. We make promises to ourselves and to others that are deeply sincere. Yet cultivating a greater appreciation of life in a sustained way, and letting it genuinely guide and direct our choices and behaviour, is often a great deal tougher than it would seem...

What's more, if we are putting off trying something new because we hope to become brave enough 'later', if we are not telling the people we like and love how much we appreciate them, if we are not healing old wounds in our own lives or between ourselves and other people, if we have no time for fun, to revel in nature, cook or write a poem, learn a language, kayak down a river or plant a garden whose mature beauty we may never see, then we are also betraying life. It is our gift so briefly. And every moment counts.

    extract from The Australian,
    Stephanie Dewrick
    May 2007

People in the mass or aggregate often have a lower intelligence than their constituent parts

Christopher Hitchens defending elitism in

'Letters to A Young Contrarian'

France, August 2000

C

as in Cars, but not excluding planes 'n boats 'n trains.

'Win at the slowest possible speed.'

*A*nyone anticipating to read something of mine would expect the subject of motor vehicles to come up. Cars are part of my DNA; all agree. Without something interesting in the driveway, I'm a lost soul. Especially a Porsche. I've had six of them and loved each one.

Now according to research I've just made up, 90% of us would have a Porsche in the garage if money didn't come into it. Which just goes to prove that 90% of people are dipsticks, because money ALWAYS comes into it. It really depends on just how you want to waste it.

There's an old technique for tuning Porsches. It's called the 'Apprentice Tune'. The keys are thrown at the workshop apprentice who dutifully hits the freeway and roars the living crap out of the car; goodbye cobwebs, hello smooth idle.

And the Fowler 1st law of mechanics – tighten it 'til it strips, then back off half a turn.

France Journal
June 2000

∿∿

Ah, the joys of Rollers, or Royces, as the purists seem to like calling them.

Lord Baden-Powell had one that all the Boy Scouts chipped in a penny each to buy him.

The Bhagwan Rajneesh received 40 of them from his devout spiritual followers.

But always the choice of heads of state and dictators around the world.

Of course, the golden rule must be remembered – consider your purchase price as the first down-payment.

And it was Henry Royce who said 'The quality remains long after the price is forgotten.'
    found in article June 2003

∿∿

'The trains themselves made me think of exile, too, for there is nothing more evocative of goodbyes than the sound, look and smell of trains. When you see people off at an airport you know they can be home again in a few hours, but a last kiss at an international railway station is like a premonition of infinity ...'
    from 'Trieste and the Meaning of Nowhere' Jan Morris
                                    France journal,
                                            June 2003

The art of picking and choosing the right motor vehicle.

To avoid:

- The ones with the blank suicide note in the glove box
- The ones for the fashionistas
- The 'weakest link' – the ones made out of lowest-bidder materials with about the same excitement as purchasing a new biro
- The car to be put on the 'definitely maybe' list
- The ones where you get the certificate confirming the owners lack of taste
- Eeny, meeny, miney, No!
- Some are a dog; some a dog with rabies
- Yes, driving the slowest common denominator transport
- The ones with dynamics not even in the field neighbouring the ballpark

♒

Clive James' description of being stuck in an airline check-in queue: 'a partial collapse of the will to live.'

♒

> The glorious thing about FI for me is that it is excessive. It is wildly wasteful and appallingly politically incorrect. It is a soap opera at 300 kph. It is Dallas with motorhomes, in which mentally unstable but often brilliant people play Monopoly with real money.
>
>   Joe Saward, 2004 (FI Afficionado + journalist)

Are the live-sheep carriers in fact U Boats?

You shouldn't be driving, when it gets to the stage that your karma runs over your dogma.

The dream to be wealthy enough to have a Bentley with an optical-prescription windscreen.
    diary 2002

On justification of purchasing a good motor car -

A piece of sculpture in the driveway will always make the journey ahead seem much more appealing.
    Found in Car
    Magazine
    June 2003

Ratty remarked solemnly to Mole: 'Believe me, my young friend, there is nothing – absolutely nothing – half so much worth doing as simply messing about in boats.'
    found in Wind in The Willows

On the Paris Metro, as noted by Kafka '…the Metro is a frail and hopeful stranger's best chance to think that he has quickly and correctly…penetrated the essence of Paris.'

Colin Jones, in his 2004 book *Paris, Biography of a City*, adds, 'In a way this is correct, yet it underestimates the extent to which Metro usage involves a certain apprenticeship. The system requires competence in a number of social rituals: buying a ticket, understanding the meaning of 'correspondence', socially correct behaviour in the presence of buskers and beggars, extremely parsimonious use of eye-contact, and so on.

It is at once the most private and individual experience – and yet also one of the most social.'

Paris journal
2007

Even in the time of high speed internet, these trains are still alarmingly fast. Twenty minutes out of Paris and you are flashing through the countryside at 250 kmh. So, why drive a Renault in French traffic at half that speed? Especially now with the first use of my Seniors Card in the TGV.

Yes, trains. Have always loved them; from Melbourne to Perth, LA to NY, Paris to Grenoble, Stockholm to the Arctic Circle and still many on the bucket list.

Train journeys are travel. Paul Theroux observed that planes in contrast are mere transfer; when you plane lands that's when your journey begins.

TGV, Paris to Auray
11/7/11

- The DC 10 is not all it's cracked up to be
- The Collins Class submarine is in a league of its own …
- Before the Wright Brothers, they said flying was impossible. It's still almost the same
- And the Spaceshuttle program – there's no such thing as a free launch
- The submarine Kursk; Vladimir Putin's unilateral if unintended attempt at world disarmament

1985. first and only adventure into boating. Together with Kent, we purchase small, almost sea-worthy outrigger canoe in Bali.

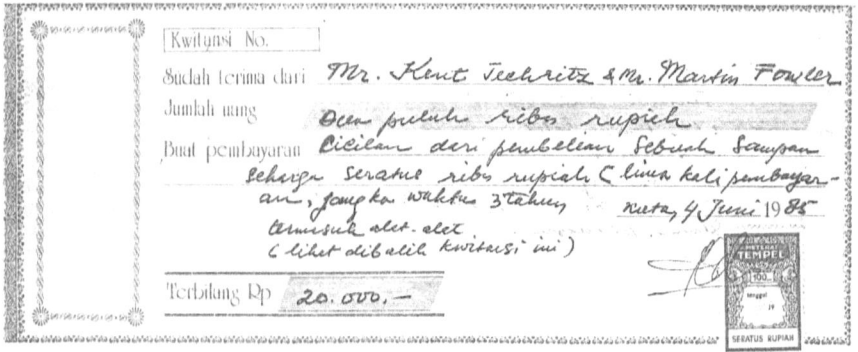

Not sure if the receipt shown was for the deposit or the full purchase price of around $20, but not a huge outlay compared to the thousands/millions spent on ocean-going craft. And not to mention the associated running costs of such yachts – likened to tearing up $50 notes under the shower!

So it's perfect we feel for the 1km trip out to surf Kuta Reef and to avoid that long paddle home.

I think it all ended in disaster on the first or second sail/paddle; mooring broke in heavy swell at the reef and our little boat unsalvageable, but never forgotten.

For posterity, thought a chronological list of my automobiles should be included for possible future reference and debates around style, logic and taste etc.

From 1968 to 1980
- Holden EH
- Land Rover
- Range Rover
- Volvo Wagon
- Lotus Elan Plus 2
- Alfetta GT
- Roven 3500 S
- Valiant Sedan

From 1981 to 1993
- Porsche 912
- Lancia HPE
- Mazda RX7
- Jaguar XJ6
- Hillman Hunter
- Daihatsu Turbo
- Porsche 924
- Holden Ute
- Mazda 323
- Falcon XY Wagon
- Rover SDI
- Porsche 911 SC
- Corvette Stingray C2

From 1994 to 1999
- Holden HT Sedan
- Holden Gemini Wagon
- Buick Electra
- Datson 280 ZX
- Honda Civic
- BMW 628
- 1977 Porsche Targa Carerra

From 2000 to 2016
- Range Rover
- Porsche Carrera 3.2
- Bentley TI
- Rolls Royce Silver Spirit
- Mitsubishi Pajero
- Ford Fairlane
- Land Rover Discovery
- Rolls Royce Silver Shadow
- Bentley Turbo R
- Porsche Cayenne Turbo
- Peugeot 308
- Fiat 500 Sport
- Fiat Freemont SUV
- Corvette C4

… to be continued I guess?

A brief chronology of the motor vehicle.

1908	good old Henry introduces the assembly line for his Model T; churns out over 16 million in the next 20 years.
1936	Italian engineer Dante Giacosa designs the Fiat 500. In 2016, it's still in the production line and I buy my first one!
1950	The FIA creates Formula 1, first race at Silverstone, UK.
1959	Austin introduces the iconic Mini. They build over 5.3 million, so it's time I consider one of the new BMW innovations.
1980	Japan dethrones the United States by becoming the world's largest producer of cars.
2016	The global car fleet reaches 1.3 billion, or one car for every six people in the world.

Tollway, freeway, highway.

One way, no way –

Outa my way!

Has to go down as one of the best days in Bali. Six am start from a flash resort in Nusa Dua. Sunrise meeting with around 50 Porsches (2 being Neil's) from Jakarta, Surabaya and Bali.

Fabulous contingency of pretty well all models, earliest being C2 right up to the latest Macan Turbo. Where else will you see 50 Porsches tagging one another through mountain passes and rainforest? And with a police motorcycle and car escort, complete with sirens.

Not forgetting the bravery of being able to swap passenger seats between Neil's 911 GTS and his Boxter S throughout the 300 km of town and country roads across beautiful Bali. Once in a lifetime experience.

Thank you Neil and Kadek.

Porsche Rally
Bali May 2016

D

as in Drink, Drank, Drunk

When I read about the evils of drinking, I gave up reading.

The Tea Ceremony

The tea ceremony gives ritual expression to the central shape of friendship; on entry, all become equal. And tranquil. Social status, economic rank and all worries are left at the door with your shoes.

The humble tasks of boiling water, pouring tea, in the calm hands of the master become exact and intimate gestures, steeped in quiet significance.

The tea ceremony is a kitchen ballet.

found in Bali 1989

You can't be a real country unless you have a beer and an airline – it helps if you have some kind of football team or some kind of nuclear weapons, but at the very least you need beer.
   Frank Zappa

Found the village of St. Martin du Fouilloux in the Loire Valley (near Angers). Feel I was probably there in a previous life, in the heart of medieval France with all its chateaux and history. But where do I find myself? At the Cointreau distillery. Enormous production from quite a small plant with beautiful copper stills and piles of dried orange peel. A moving, religious experience standing in front of 300,000 litres of my precious liquor that they have been producing for around 150 years.

France
June 1997

Oh yes, where would we be without alcohol? A wonderful preservative and social lubricant that can have so many far-reaching effects and lead to so many problems.

Managed properly, two things can be avoided – Methyphobia (the fear of alcohol) and bottle fatigue (hangovers). However, the drink problem that I'm developing is that I can't afford it. It hasn't helped either by me being a social drinker, where you say 'so shall I' every time someone has a drink.

But at least I know I'm not an alcoholic. Alcoholics go to meetings. After this trip to France though, I intend going back to start a home group, Drinkers Unanimous; if you don't feel like a drink, you ring another member and they come over to persuade you.

> *The Problem with the world is that everyone is a few drinks behind.*
>
> Humphrey Bogart

Of course, social drinking is better than not drinking at all. The problem with not drinking is that when you wake in the morning, you know that's the best you will feel all day.

So, enjoy your alcohol. Whether it's beer in cans, Cairns or Cannes, it all tastes good. But remember, you don't buy beer, you rent it. Wine with every meal, well most meals; a meal without wine is called 'breakfast'. And I enjoy cooking with wine – sometimes I even put it in the food.

Paris 2004

Long, long ago, when the idle rich deserved their description and had time and servants to spare, it was customary to change for cocktails and dinner after a day of country pursuits. 'Let's get out of these wet clothes,' as Robert Benchley used to say, 'and into a dry martini.'

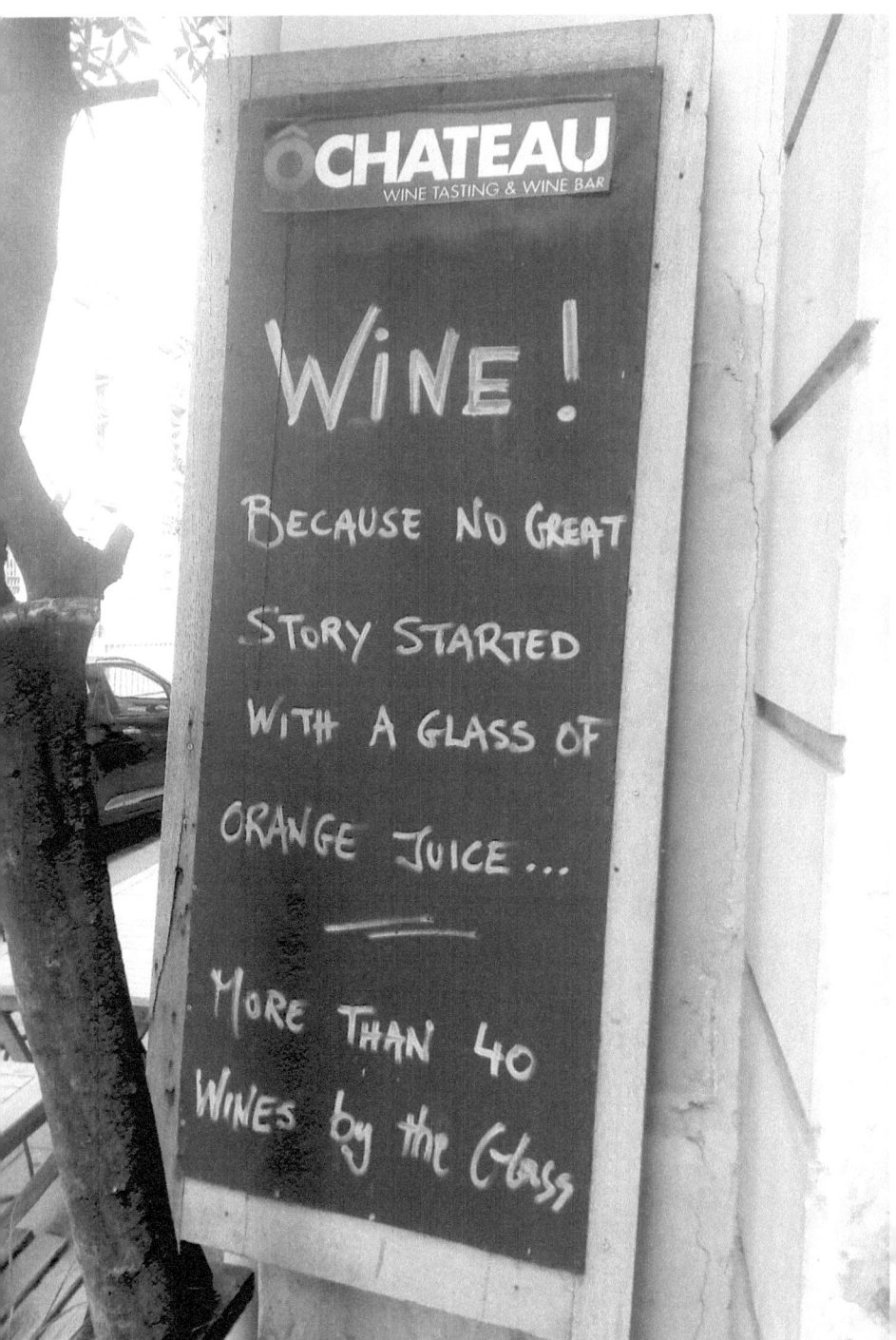

Nice sign outside Paris wine bar 2016

E

as in

Entertainment, TV,
Radio and Film

What's not; the 35 channels of Hawaiian cable TV and the CNN News, coming 'at you' and not to you – if it bleeds, it leads. from journal What's hot and What's not.

Hawaii July 1999

༄

Some Australian movies are very moving; I move out of the theatre when they come on.

France journal 1999

༄

TV's naturalism, the bland sequential account of life, may look convincing, but it's not how we experience things. Our minds constantly mix the 'real' with the imaginary, 'fact' with fantasy, the present with the past and future. In our subconscious, we are forever sifting, hypothesising, cross-referencing, rehearsing and remembering – in a chaotic, kaleidoscopic, nonsensical flood of thoughts ...

    Phillip Adams, 1991

༄

Pay Television, or Free to Air-head TV as a medium? Both just like a medium steak; neither rare nor well-done.

Paris 2004

༄

'*If you don't read a newspaper, you're never a day behind.*'
    Found in 'Falling Man' by Don DeLillo

... The commercial marketplace has always been a place where consumers do more than make a series of rational decisions about products and services they need to buy. The marketplace beckons with its promise of colour and movement, and consumers respond with pleasure. We are often shopping for the experience as well as for the merchandise; we watch the ads for fun as well as for information; our purchases are driven by a combination of rational and emotional factors, and the emotional factors usually prevail...//

... Advertising is capitalism's servant, not its architect. It makes a legitimate, if modest, contribution to the total workings of a free enterprise economy ...//

The critics of advertising have often imbued it with more significance than is warranted. It is actually a relatively weak marketing tool, struggling to compete with the consumer's personal experience, the recommendations of friends, the price cuts of competitors, the free samples, in-store displays and demonstrations that appeal more directly to the customer ...//

... Advertising will always attract criticism, of course, because we don't always admire what we see in the mirror it holds up to our society. Its very existence reminds us that we are sometimes greedy, selfish, competitive and materialistic; we sometimes make foolish and irrational purchases; we clutter our lives with stuff that contradicts the values we claim to espouse ...//

Yet it also invites us to have fun and, sometimes, to engage in a little self indulgence that is mostly harmless and may actually be therapeutic. After all, if you've already decided to buy a car or a tub of margarine, or a power suit, where's the harm in Toyota, Flora or Max Mara trying to tug you in the direction of theirs?

    extract from The Age 10/1/04 by Hugh MacKay

French film – spare, elegant and exact as only the French can be.

Paris 2002

I'd rather brush with ordinary toothpaste and have 20% fewer commercials.

And France's television? Just as banal as we see everywhere. Flicking through 60 odd channels over the last six weeks, nothing but mindless variety shows, the ubiquitous game shows and the usual garden variety sitcoms, you soon realise that French television breaks no new ground – the interesting programmes on at impossible times and the boring ones always when you are winding down after the day. Yes, the good old television – shaping our lives and changing society ever so gradually over the years.

Paris, August 2006

I pity the French cinema because it has no money. I pity the American cinema because it has no ideas.

director, Jean-luc Godard

Marc is in love with Sophie, Sophie loves Francois, Francois has the hots for Charlotte, who is in love with Isabelle. But Isabelle loves Gerard, who has a crush on Florence, who loves Marc. And in the end they all go out to dinner.

Hollywood takes the piss on French film scripts.

found in Paris, July 2008

'... the case of a comedian who, after years of psychotherapy finally understood the reasons why he needed to be funny; and having understood, stopped.'

Julian Barnes' 'Nothing to Be Frightened Of'

F

as in France

'I had two affairs in my life: Paris and the ocean.'
– Victor Hugo

Paris est le monde,
le reste de la terre n'est
rien d'autre que
sa banlieues
Mariavaux, 1734
(Paris is the world, the rest of the earth is nothing but it's suburbs.)
France Journal
July 2007

'... Then I sat in a little park in Pl. Paul-Painleve and dreamily watched a curving row of beautiful rosy tulips, rigid and swaying fat shaggy sparrows, beautiful short haired mademoiselles strolling by. It's not that French girls are beautiful, it's their cute mouths and the sweet way they talk French (their mouths pout rosily), the way they've perfected the short haircut and the way they amble slowly when they walk, with great sophistication, and of course their chic way of dressing and undressing. Paris, a stab in the heart finally.'

from short story 'Big Trip to Europe' Jack Kerouac
Paris journal, summer 1998

Well, France – a country famous for coffee. And it doesn't even produce it. Great to be here. Breathe in a few Parisienne diesel fumes, step around the dog turds, avoid the prostitutes and head for coffee and croissant. God! $8 – jut as well I didn't take the OJ as well. But as somebody said, don't look at it as an overpriced coffee, think of it as rent. You can spend two hours at that footpath table, just soaking up the sun and atmosphere, watching, writing, reading.

Then head for the Balajo café on the rue de Lappe. From the '30s and still has original décor and I don't think the ashtrays have been emptied from when I was there three years ago. Edith Piaf got married here. It's just the Balajo. There's a Paris saying, 'One day everyone will have been to, will come to, or is coming to the Balajo'
    Paris journal
    June 1997

〜〜

*B*ack in Paris. All the world's a café! Just watch the endless human types walk past. Old French ladies with their dogs, Chinese girls, suited bankers heading for The Bourse, serious thinkers with berets, serious dressers, piano-accordian players with drooping moustaches, pretty girls sitting applying their war-paint, large African women in vibrant tent dresses.

Read in café, 'Yes I lick man now – anagram of Monica Lewinsky'
Paris journal
Summer 1998

〜〜

Well, put a ferret on my nose and call me Gerard Depardieu, I'm back here for the third year in a row! Must be something here and quite a contrast from the 'brash and flash' of New York.

Maybe it's the pretty French girls or 'Bien Foutue' (well built) as you can't affectionately call them.

Yes, Paris – a stab in the heart. Where the reality matches the dream. You never tire of it, despite the noise, traffic and crowds.

History in live performance.

Ah, the enviable position of having my feet in Australia and my head in France.

I'm back here at my favourite hotel. Full of character and characters in my hotel – the Hotel Le Grunge. Why, it's so run down, vandals broke in and did thousands of Francs worth of improvements. You have to wipe your feet each time before you go out …

Observations this year:

- Stephane tells me that 6 million cellular phones were sold in the last 12 months. And you can see this in the street from last year – every man and his mistress seem to have one.
- The internet is not yet popular, but it's slowly creeping in.
- They still haven't properly repaired the tunnel where Di died.
- And the French don't like America's involvement in Kosovo – NATO referred to as the 'New American Terrorist Organisation'
- Xabi gives me the Quotation of The Week to use (when required) 'Je vous trouve vraiment tres belle'

France Journal
July 1999

※

Paris is an ocean. Sound it: you will never touch bottom. Survey it, report on it! However scrupulous your surveys and reports, however numerous and persistent the explorers of this sea may be, there will always remain virgin places, undiscovered caverns, flowers, pearls, monsters and there will always be something extraordinary.

Honore de Balzac 1834

※

17 June 2004

*H*aving just spent time in New York and London, where everything appears to be organised chaos, a huge sigh of relief and gratification to know that there can be beauty and order in a huge city.

Dinner with Fabiola, Republique, reveals she has lost none of her love of life and incredible energy and vitality. Single and happy with her destiny and dedicated to her writing and investigative journalism. The most lovely girl in all respects.

Reading Milan Kundera's *Life is Elsewhere*. Borrowing one of his phrases, possibly all of these writings are how I have wanted to express the rather vague notion of the sadness and vanity of life. Life is elsewhere.

And the people you see 'dressed in the kind of clothes worn only to avoid walking around naked' (from the same book).

'This is why some animals eat their young'. Comment by bystander watching a misbehaving child.

Suresnes
24 July 2006

*D*on't think I've ever stood in the one place for so long. Champs Elysees. Finish of the Tour de France. Arrived early yesterday at 11am to be greeted by big crowds already lining the barricades. Secured one of the last spots, and a good one. Some had camped the night. After 2 hours standing, the crowd had doubled, after 3 hours it had tripled.

By race time, it was 10 deep the full length of the avenue, lots of Australian flags too. By 4pm, I was so tired and footsore that it didn't matter that the race was running another 1 hour later than anticipated!

But all worth it when the pelaton rounded the top of the Champs Elysees to start their 8 finishing laps – just as many motorcycles and back-up vehicles (approximately 100!) all in the convoy.

Great day, and don't the French just love their cycling. Over 3,700,000 bicycles were sold in 2005!

France journal
2006

So what is it that brings me back to France for maybe the 10th summer? This was raised by my good Basque friend, Xavier who reminded me over a glass of wine that it was 10 years ago in 1997 that we met over a beer in Vietnam, later to meet up in Paris again the next month for what has become the annual 'Tiger gathering'.

France. So what is all the fuss about? Surely it can't just be the food and wine, the cafés, the architecture or the elegance and history of the whole damn place?

No, it's to do with the French themselves. Impossible to categorise them. They're as warm and cold, as rude and welcoming, as obstinate and accommodating as all of us; all trying to live, work and love, and at the same time making out some sense and order of their place in a quickly changing world.

It's when you meet people who are willing, though not too hastily, to share with you their lives and experiences, no matter how varied, touching and ridiculous some of it might be, that you know your travels are being enriched and challenged.

I have been so very fortunate to have lived and breathed France; from the various apartments of Xavier and Laetitia in Paris, from the farmhouse and rural villages of Brittany with Gaelle and Hugues, from the power of The Alps and the chateau 'Grand Verger' at Theys with Thierry and Christine, and the rustic charm and comradeship of the Pays Basque with Xavier's family.

It is Gertrude Stein's comment in 1932 that clears things up: 'It isn't so much what France gives you, as what it doesn't take away.'

Paris journal, Montmartre
August 2007

My 2007 Definitive Guide to Etiquette and Survival in Paris.

(can be updated daily)

1. Leave cargo pants, t-shirts with slogans and bumbags at home.
2. Wear shoes that you have to apply polish to.
3. Speak quietly. American and Australian English carries.
4. Avoid the $10 coffees. The French do.
5. Never eat cheese before meals. Always before dessert though.
6. Put your bread on the table. There are no bread plates; you know that that plastic tablecloth is ultra clean!
7. Speak a little French.
8. Give some change to the homeless in the Métro.
9. Step on the occasional dog turd. The French do.
10. Forget low-fat and organic – perfectly useless here.
11. Remember, there is no French word for 'diet'.
12. Eat your mussels with an empty mussel shell and not your fork.
13. Be rude in department stores – the staff (who are usually rude) expect it. It's a game to them with their policy being the 'customer is always wrong'.
14. Never wear a bike helmet. The French don't. The police don't. Why mess up your hair?

15. Sit and read on park benches after sleeping in all morning.
16. Don't go to every museum.
17. Drink wine every day and put ice in your rosé. The French do.
18. Watch movies you don't understand.
19. Listen to new French music on the headphones in FNAC and Virgin shops.
20. Sing in the Métro.
21. Adopt an 'Amelie' sense of the ridiculous
22. Jump the Métro barrier for that last train at night.
23. Leave that map at home some days.
24. Kiss on both cheeks, right then left. Possibly right again.
25. As with licking your knife, don't wipe your plate with your bread.
26. Eat things you wouldn't at home – feel comfortable with foie gras and snails on your plate
27. Do things you wouldn't do at home.
28. _____ add your suggestion.

*H*ow can you tire of Paris? It has survived 4 revolutions to date and there's the possibility of being able to watch the next one on the internet!

With over 300 kms of tunnels underneath and 13 kms of river on top flowing past some of the best architecture available, Paris has more to offer than one lifetime can accommodate. Thousands of cafes, bistros and brasseries. And around 1300 bakeries for you to separate the wheat from the chaff! Add to this the 400 parks and gardens, 140 theatres, 2 opera houses, 350 cinemas, and the covered passageways from 1820 (which were unfortunately the start of shopping centres).

But after six weeks, you start feeling that it's time to leave. You've been snubbed by waiters. You've paid exorbitant prices for mediocre meals. Have been laughed at for your French. Had one too many limp salads. People constantly smoking next to you before, after and during meals. You have stood in another dog turd. You have again stepped out into oncoming traffic coming on the right. Another piece of yesterday's baguette for breakfast; another aching 200 or so steps from Montmartre down to my Métro.

Yes, it's feeling like time to leave – but then! A small amusing incident will happen on the street. You turn around and make eye contact with a girl with an umbrella who has witnessed the same thing. You both smile at one another. It's then you get that little jolt telling you … telling you that although, yes, it is time to leave Paris, that you are really never going to leave.

There is no other.

Montmartre
August 2007

≈≈

I arrived in Paris just too late last year for my beloved 'beach' along the Seine. It had been pulled up and put in storage (where do all those tonnes of sand go?).

But plenty of time this year to grab a deck chair and book and watch the world go by. It is never the same; last year rainy and overcast, overcast faces to match. Now, 30° as you have your bag and sunscreen searched by police at the entrances. Military patrols with assault weapons mingling with the bikinis, vendors and children, music and dancing. A city under siege, but the 'beachgoers' seem quite relaxed.

The Government 'Be Nice to Tourists' programme introduced several years ago seems to be working. Most service industry folk still however abide by the 'customer is always wrong' principle, but there is a noticeable change in manner.

And refreshing to see smoking, sunglasses and small dogs still in fashion. This is evident outside as well.

The e-cigarette is slowly showing signs of acceptance, but does nothing for the yellow ceilings and dirty ashtrays that we've come to enjoy. Perhaps a future 'i Cigarette' may address this problem?

Paris
August 2016

G

as in global

(think warming,
financial, terrorism)

France journal
August 2000

Found in Australian Review of Books, June 2000
Book review by Kevin Hart, on 4 books by E.M. Cioran – Tears & Saints; On The Heights of Despair; The Trouble With Being Born; All Gall Is Divided.

'What is it in Cioran that attracts people these days? Perhaps it is in the sense of homelessness that his writing evokes so powerfully...

The world has changed immeasurably since Cioran wrote, yet with each move closer to complete globalisation everyone loses more sense of home. Whether we like it or not, whether we travel or stay put, we are all destined to live in America. Today, we do not leave home, it is home that leaves us.'

My great grandfather got it right. When asked to predict what the weather was going to be like in the future, he replied 'Unpredictable'.

Paris journal 2005

'The most effective attacks against globalisation are usually not those related to economics. Instead, they are social, ethical and above all, cultural.

... The allegations against globalisation and in favour of cultural identity reveal a static conception of culture that has no historical basis. Which cultures have ever remained identical and unchanged over time?

... Globalisation extends radically to all citizens of this planet the possibility to construct their individual cultural identities through voluntary action, according to their preferences and intimate motivations ...

The fear of Americanisation of the planet is more ideological paranoia than reality. There is no doubt that with globalisation English has become the language of our time, as was Latin in the Middle Ages. And it will continue its ascent, since it is an indispensable instrument for international transactions and communications.

But does this mean that English necessarily develops at the expense of the other great languages? Absolutely not. In fact, the opposite is true. The vanishing of borders, and an increasingly independent world, have created incentives for new generations to learn and assimilate to other cultures ...

Cultures must live freely, constantly jousting with other cultures. This renovates and renews them, allowing them to evolve and adapt to the continuous flow of life ...

Globalisation will not make local cultures disappear; in a framework of worldwide openness, all that is valuable and worthy of survival in local cultures will find fertile ground in which to bloom ...

National cultures were often forged in blood and fire, prohibiting the teaching or participation of vernacular languages or the practice of religions and customs that dissented from those the nation-state considered ideal ...

But, contrary to the warnings of those who fear globalisation, it is not easy to completely erase cultures, however small they may be, if behind them is a rich tradition and people who practice them, even if in secret. And today, thanks to the weakening of the nation-state, we are seeing forgotten, marginalised and silenced local cultures re-emerging and displaying dynamic signs of life in the great concert of this globalised planet.

>   Some notes on Globalisation, from extract by Mario Vargas Llosa
>   February 2001

Here's a few despots to avoid around the world, who have left their not so proud mark in many places:

- The Bhagwan Rajneesh
- David Koresh of The Branch Davidians
- The Amanda Marga sect
- Jim Jones of Jonestown
- Luc Jouret (Switzerland)
- L. Ron Hubbard
- David Duke, the KKK
- The Children of God
- Oral Roberts + Jimmy Swaggart
- Jimmy + Tammy Bakker

Journal, New York
2005

'... many French people are preoccupied by the fear of being Americanised. In the 1950s and 1960s the desire for prosperity was such that American business methods were eagerly copied; 'management' became a French word.

Foreign investment in France increased so that about one quarter of French industry in now foreign-owned, and half of that quarter belongs to American investors.

The comic strip, which has been an unusually important artistic and intellectual form, owes a great deal to MAD (where Goscinny, the inventor of Asterix, once worked).

The French popular music business ... is now 90% in the hands of US firms ... At least one third of French television is American, and one third of films shown in cinemas ...'

> some comments on the Americanisation of France,
> from 'The French' by Theodore Zeldin, 1983

Paris journal 2007

It is with travel and globalisation too that we recognize our own foreignness; most clearly when in flight and away from home.

The instability of meaning and the difficulty of translation between generations within, as well as across, different cultures and nationalities, all help us put the world into a better perspective.

OK, we lose some of our traditions – social, religious, language etc., but these can also be constraints on our development. For the greater part of history we have had limited access to other cultures and regions, but with plane travel, television and the internet we now all experience great diversity.

So, nothing but excitement for this new era. Bring me an air ticket!
Hawaii 2011

On money troubles in transit

I know the Australian economy is pretty sound and that our dollar's weakness is due to a large part in the strong $US. But, hey, try travelling with this – it's killing me here in France.

In 1974, the $A was worth $US1.40, so it's had a 25 year slide till now! From 66cents in January, to 48c in April and now 52 cents. Crippling.

But experts were predicting not so long back that it would be up over 70 cents now. As one economist has put it, 'all the people with all the know-how, they don't have a clue. It's got a lot to do with sentiment and our currency is tiny by world standards – we represent only 2-3% of the world's economic output.'

So, gather your small change, buy a baguette, some cheese and a coffee and ride out the storm in the hope of a cheaper France next year.
France journal 12 August 2002

My Paris Agreement

2016

Keep calm. Drink champagne. Catherine Overington commented in one of her excellent articles in The Australian, that the world is not perfect, but it comes pretty close.

Every generation has had fears to contend with – famine, war, pollution etc. For now, we are faced with global warming and climate change, Yes, we are addressing these, but I'm not sure how sensibly. Like previous generational scares, are our climate fears being overly exaggerated by scientists and politics of the day?

Sure, the planet is warming, as it has through various phases of history and some of this is certainly attributed to us. But how much? Australia emits around 550 million tonnes of CO_2 per year and yet the world's volcanoes emit more than this, but have never been shown to cause detectable global warming. Time to re-evaluate?

We are also warned of the sea-level rises, but again, will they have the catastrophic outcomes we are led to believe? Truth seems to be from a modelled study that a sea-level rise of 6 meters say over a period of 100 years would inundate about 16,000 square miles of coastline and displace almost 6% of the world's population. As most of these 400 million live in the cities, the relocation would only involve around 15 million and this over the projected time frame of 100 years. Not exactly calamitous.

So, keep calm.

I was around in the '70's when overpopulation, scarce food and water, pollution – all were going to wipe out the human race, the whole 3 billion of us!

Now we have reached 7.5 billion with the majority being fed and watered and few in the poorer countries actually starving or living in extreme poverty.

We are doing ok, eating better, smoking less and living longer. In the last 30 years, life expectancy has increased from 63 years to 72 years. Something like 90% of all children are in school, pay gaps are closing and many diseases are now well controlled with effective and affordable vaccines.

So, yes, keep calm and live and act responsibly; it's not all as bad as we are led to believe, trust me.

Saigon-Paris flight
August 2016

H

as in History

'What good is there to
weep over parts of life?
The whole of it calls
for tears.'
– Seneca

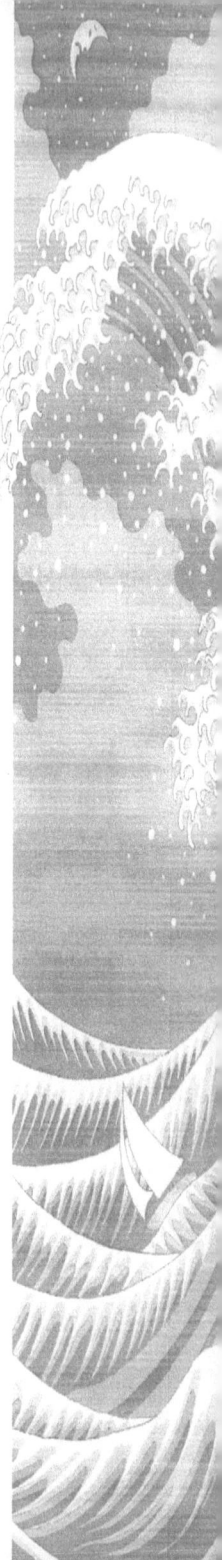

Stop! Beyond here is the Empire of Death. Or words to that effect. This is the greeting at the entrance to the Paris Catacombs. Cheery little place to visit when the cars, costs and chaos of the city have to be escaped. Take the Métro to 1, Pl. Denfert – Rochereau. Observe the majestic lion guarding the place, created by the same sculptor of the Statue of Liberty. Pay your francs, suspend normal breathing and descend 20 metres into the myriad of tunnels that were the quarries of the building stones of the city. When the Left Bank all looked like caving in around 1810, the city engineers stopped the digging. The tunnels then became the housing for the bodies and remains from the city's other overcrowded cemeteries. Supposedly the tunnels also became the headquarters for the Resistance fighters in World War Two. Paris looks different when you come back up into the sunlight.

Paris journal
August 2000

In March 1886, Van Gogh moved from Holland to Paris, where he took an apartment at 54 rue Lepic, a market street that winds up from Bde de Clichy towards the top of Montmartre's butte.

Here, he painted views over the rooftops, with the gas lamps that still give the area so much of its character. He captured the atmosphere of La Guinguette, now the renamed Auberge de la Bonne Franquette at 18 rue St. Rustique, the restaurant so typical of the many that crowd around the Pl. du Tertre.

Lyon
August 2000

'History isn't was. History is. No matter how much we wipe our feet at the front door, we track history through the house. Leaving its muddy, bloody footprints all over the carpet.

... History is ... the passing of time is truly terrifying, dragging all of us to our deaths. Yet its passing makes existence bearable. Time dulls most memories and erases many in their entirety, so that entire civilisations, their atrocities and their achievements, erode, corrode and disappear forever ...

... History and time don't have much to do with each other. Just as Hitler, Stalin, Mao Zedong, Pol Pot and innumerable other despots and monsters are still alive for millions who suffered at their hands, so are the individuals who haunt our private lives. So are the people we've lost and loved. Long-ago emotions can return with an intensity, and urgency, that truly astonishes. For Marcel Proust, the trigger was the taste of a Madeleine. For you, it might be the mention of a name, the smell of a penny, the glimpse of a view, a few bars of a song.

... More and more we live in a world of all-at-once-ness. We are trained to have shorter attention spans, to focus on the seductions of the moment, the shock of the new, the bombardment of distractions.

... Whether we know it or not, history's illness can be seen and heard and felt in every scrap of our behaviour, our beliefs, our prejudices, our popular culture. For there is history in every note of music, in every word we utter, in every tool we use or artefact we own.

History is. And if it isn't, it bloody well should be. God knows it's hard to live with our histories, personal and collective. But it would be even worse to live, to try to live, without them. History is our burden and our inheritance. Our curse and our glory. It is our explanation.'

> From Phillip Adams, 'History is now, not later'
> France Journal, July 2001

'Kerouac was 40 when *Big Sur* was published and I was a babe in arms. I am 40 now and reread *Big Sur* and see not hidden things that had passed me by in my young lumber-jacketed enthusiasm, but something I could not have possibly known then.

It is the terrible familiarity of the gathered years, of the life lived, of time wasted, drinks drunk, passivity of the heart turned to anger. It is the horrifying snapshot of life wringing out a sensitive and creative soul. A merciless window into what could be.

Big Sur may have inspired a writing life more than 20 years ago, but what has it become now, sitting quietly on the shelf? A warning. And quite possibly a life raft.'

> Matt Condon, Australian writer on Jack Kerouac
> New York Journal
> July 2002

Some of the 101 Gadgets that Changed My World.

helped by the Popular Mechanics suggestions July 2011

1. MOBILE/SMART PHONES
   The most widely used gadget. The first billion sold in 20 years, the second billion in 4 and the third billion in 2!

2. RADIOS
   Since 1938, the first instrument of instant mass communication.

3. MUSIC MACHINES
   How else would we have enjoyed such a spread of different musical genres? The phonograph, the transistor, the cassette, the Walkman, the CD, the MP3, the iPod.

4. ELECTRIC GUITAR
   Leo Fender designed the first in 1951, when Keith Richards was 8.

5. SUNGLASSES
   Fashion and function from the New Jersey boardwalk, 1929.

6. CALCULATOR
   Always have been and will be hopeless at maths.

7. SWISS ARMY KNIFE/LEATHERMAN
   Now, everyone was a mechanic

8. SAFETY RAZOR
   Saving hours every week since 1918.

9. CHAINSAW
   Once to cut down forests, now to cut up firewood in the back yard.

10. CAN OPENER
    The bachelor's best friend since 1958.

11. TEFLON PAN
    The bachelors 2nd best friend since 1961.

12. MICROWAVE
    The bachelors 3rd best friend since 1967.

13. SUPER SOAKER
    The most powerful model, 1lt per second up to 15 metres! Have wrought backyard mayhem since 1990.

14. _____
    Insert your favourite

Hawaii Journal 2011

I

as in islands and Indonesia

'Wherever you go,
there you are.'
– Buckaroo Banzai

WHAT'S HOT
- Boxters + the new VW Beetle
- Cigars seem more popular, reflecting the general upturn in the economy.
- Shops, restaurants and hotels appear less busy, reflecting the Japanese economy.
- Bourbon and Gin on special at $7.99
- Elvis still alive and well
- Donna has been at the desk of my Royal Grove Hotel since 1985!
- footnote: she is still there this stay, 2014!

WHAT'S ROT
- The 35 channels of Cable TV
- Drive-by burgers and shootings; 'Would you like a box of shells with that?'
- Korean small cars posing serious threat to American chrome
- And on an ad for root beer – 'You want just any root beer coming out your nose when you laugh?'
- And, in Bali, the best way to prevent infection caused by biting insects? Just don't bite any.
- And after drinking Indonesian whiskey? Your mouth tastes like a Garuda in-flight blanket the next morning.
- And you ask the Hawaiians if they have a word for 'menyana'. They reply that they have but it is a word that does not have the same urgency …

from my 'What's Hot and What's Rot' journal entry, Hawaii July 1999

First journal, first overseas trip, flew out of Sydney 30th December 1973 to Jakarta, for what was to become an ongoing love affair with Indonesia, its people and the friends I have made there over the last 40 years.

A few extracts to put these travel days in perspective.

- 30.12.73 Exchanged $US at the Jakarta airport on arrival – Rp413 to the $US. City accommodation that night at the Green Door Hostel, Rp450 and beer Rp200.
- 1.1.74 Half hour walk along train line to catch train to Jogjakarta – twelve hours in 3rd class. All hostels full on arrival, so ended up on mattress on floor of hostel office.
- 6.1.74 Took bus in direction of remote village of Patjitan on the Javanese south coast. Had to ride on the roof of the bus with others as seats inside all taken. Turned out that I and my American travel companion were first westerners to travel this route. Bus only went as far as village of Praji. Tremendous excitement as the 50 or so children who surrounded us had not seen westerners before – many crying in fright, many fascinated by our white skin until local police detained us, took our passports and demanded that we hand over our firearms! After explaining that we were tourists and inventing story about being there on 'research', they bundled us onto a truck with five locals carrying rifles. Things getting a little tense at this stage, until our 'guards' turn out to be bird hunters and they drive us to our destination, now all smiling and laughing and, like us, not really knowing what was going on.
- 10.1.74 Completed 16 hour bus trip from Java to Bali, so overnighted in Denpasar hotel. Early morning bimo to Kuta and walk down dirt road for first look at the magnificent palm fringed Kuta Beach.
- 16.1.74 Moved into Losmen at Legian Beach, a few kilometres down a dirt road through farmland – quiet

and peaceful after Kuta. Nowhere to really eat, so walked back to Kuta at sunset to Mama's Restaurant for great vegie burger and iced juice.

- 19.1.74 Biggest surf for days! A battle to get out past the shore break, but only 4 in the water and so many waves to pick from and share. Out again at sunset after watching Holden being towed out of the sand.
- Good meal of fish, salad and jam pancakes for Rp475 for dinner. Price included a beer.
- 22.1.74 Reflections on Java and Bali as I wait for Pan Am 812 return flight home
  » Regret not learning more Indonesian language before trip.
  » Early nights advisable as chooks, dogs, workers all on the go around 4:30am.
  » Water bottle and tablets essential as you soon get sick of the soft drinks and paying for them
  » If possible, though doubtful, try and like eating Durian fruit. Apparently goodness-packed but obnoxious in taste, odour and texture.
  » Beaches not as nice as home, but the black sand and palm trees along Kuta still very appealing. Beaches really clean, no flies, bottles or rubbish, but dangerous rips to be careful of.
  » Kuta by far the biggest tourist trap- filled with losmens, food stalls, restaurants, clothes stores, batik sellers, postcard sellers – can really get you down after a while.
  » Legian a much better deal, only a few kilometres down the beach – a couple of losmens and 2 food stalls. Much larger concentration of drugs though which tends to spoil it.
  » Swallow your malaria tablets quickly, as taste is really vile.

Bali journal 1974

Melbourne – Central Australia – Bali, 1976

After months of planning, we all finally arrived at 6:00am at the hangar of Southern Air Services, Moorabbin Airport.

Myself, Renate Neurich, Bill Mann, Bruce MacIntosh, Clive Brookes and our pilot Don Sowman; Don to fly us in the twin engine Piper Aztec across Central Australia to Bali.

31.1.76 Off on schedule at 7:30am and rough flight to Mildura for refuel. Arrive Ayers Rock late afternoon for fantastic sunset.

1.8.76 Sleep on floor of airport alongside Rock and up for early start to do the climb. Leave late AM for amazing low-level flight across desert.

2.8.76 Day in Broome due to Customs formalities and life raft requirement to cross ocean.

3.8.76 Uncomfortable night before sleeping on seating at Broome airport passenger lounge. Trouble free 5.5 hour flight across beautiful blue ocean to Bali. Usual painful passage through Indonesian Customs after being landed on wrong runway and down-wind by not-so-smart airport control. Don certainly let this be known to officials, who naturally weren't concerned.

4.8.76-11.8.76

Good vibes all along through Bali. Island full of French this month. Bicycle hire for Rp200 a day; fruit salads; sunsets; full moon and high, high tides; extra big swells!; bintangs + turtle soups; 'The Pub' run by Fred; sell, sell, sell; temples and dances; coconut oil massages; peace.

12.8.76 Detained 3 hours at Bali Customs and 2 hours at Broome Customs due to 600kg hash haul from light plane a few days before. Inspection panels of plane all unbolted and thorough searches luckily revealed nothing. Another restless night sleeping at Broome airport passenger terminal, only to be woken at 3:30am with small jet touching down!

13.8.76 Good flight from Broome to Tennant Creek for refuel and tuck into cold milkshakes, sorely missed in Bali. Arrived Alice Springs by nightfall.

14.8.76 All day flight back home to Melbourne with refuel on way at Leigh Creek. MCG and suburbs a far cry from the desert landscapes!

Bali journal 1976

(This included and dedicated to the memory of Don Sowman our pilot. Tragically killed several years later in a crop dusting accident.)

〰️

Two hour walk to airport to say goodbye to Lilik at Jimbaran, sad not to see her smile again now for a while. Decided to return to Kuta by walking around the ocean side of the runway. This proved not too difficult, and amazing to be standing in front of the runway with a 747 bearing down on you – all flaps, wheels and landing lights blaring.

And then to be met by Spanish drum tutor, Vidal and German girl, Jasmin who both had paddled around the runway in kayak. Had drum lessons and I owe him mangoes in lieu of payment. Must look for Lombok drum.

〰️

S trange days. Jasmin met on beach Legian, minus drum. Travelling on her own and takes up invitation to stay at Sri Beach Inn and for some travelling. Pack luggage (and drum). Next morning head off at 4:30am for sunrise at Mt. Batur and then up the coast to Medewi. Good to see Ketut again at his family's bungalows and warung + book for the next two nights. Surf, sun and good times and Jasmin proves the ultimate Girl Friday, sitting on a deserted beach, playing drum, much to amusement of a few kids and timber cutters who congregate around us. Given a coconut as a gift of friendship which we share back at Ketut's – don't forget to squeeze the juice of one lemon into the coconut water.

31.8.93
Bali journal

TAMAN SARI COTTAGES

Wayan Ledang and family invite you to stay at **Taman Sari Cottages**, Seminyak. Situated only a short walk from magnificent Seminyak Beach, the cottages provide inexpensive quiet, open - air living, yet are within easy reach of the best restaurants and shops on Bali.

* Thatched roof Balinese - style cottages, double storey, each with the privacy of a tropical garden and landscaped outdoor living area.
* Fully serviced with private bathroom, refrigerator, stove and bedroom fan, your cottage will be cleaned daily and fresh linen is provided.
* Laundry and ironing service is available.
* Breakfast and light snacks provided if required.
* Safe deposit for valuables.
* Tours and transport can be arranged to your requirements with car, motor cycle and bicycles for hire.
* Surfing and fishing trips arranged.
* Free transfers Airport / Cottages / Airport by our vehicle (15 minutes).

An alternative Bali?

Yes, there is a lot of Bali left. The _real_ Bali.

Where streams wander idly through lush green ricefields and rainforest. Where unridden waves break on empty beaches and disappear into the gritty sand.

Where the pattern has not been disturbed and things are like they always have been.

So come and explore it with us. But don't bring too much with you to clutter your mind. Don't expect all the conveniences that are on tap in the city either.

The food is fresh, healthy and just good. Spicy rice, vegetables and fresh seafood flavoured by coconut, ginger and peanuts.

There are no weather forecasts. It will be hot, rainy, sunny, humid, cool cloudy and everything else. But you will be able to feel it. See it. Taste it, hear it and live it.

Somehow in western civilization we seem to be losing all sense of proportion and balance and life passes us by very quickly.

Well, it doesn't work that way in Bali.

Come and find out.

Flyer for my Bali cottages, 1988

All journeys are one and the same. They all begin with us leaving home with an idea, a hope, a dream of something; they all end with our returning somehow changed – a broken board, a broken heart, a scar, a memory of perfection. If you travel enough, the beginnings and ends begin to blur and run together like watercolours, and the dreams and memories become one, indistinguishable.

Bali journal 1994

There appears to be a marvellous assimilation of aboriginal islanders, US mainlanders, US dropouts, Japanese, Filipinos and no outward appearance of racism.

Big cars, big meals, hire anything from a boogie board to a $400k Lamborghini at $1100 a day. Corvettes in their natural habitat and priced correctly.

Catchphrase heard in Waikiki, 'Don't grumble, be humble'.

Hawaii journal
September 1997

August 2000

Postcards Near the Edge

All this trip, through Hawaii, Cal, NY, France, Paris and now Bali, have been haunted by a line from *The Talented Mr Ripley* – 'I always thought it would be better to be a fake somebody than a real nobody'. And cafes are the new 'look-out towers' in the human game park, watching the fake somebodies jostling for position with the real nobodies at 'feeding and breeding' time; mobile phoneys.

Yes, they are all out there. The freaks and geeks, the pizza butts, the nuts and sluts, the haves and the have-mores. Lovely description of business suits in NY – 'white collar overalls'. And the Italians in Bali – 'barracudas in paradise' could become the next televisual feast for those at home of an evening?

But, you have to love California. All those real nobodies trying all sorts of ways to turn them from the startlingly ordinary into the breathtakingly improbable beauties that Hollywood demands.

So, whatever happened to grace, gravitas and grey hair? Everyone clinging onto youth, seeing the aging process as 'a life running out, rather than a life filling up'.

Woman going under the knife to be stitched into the semblance of youth.

Trying to achieve everything before our 'use-by-date' comes up. No longer moving through life in measured stages as previous generations did.

We spend our childhoods wanting to grow up and waiting to be adults, and when there, devote a lot of time on discussing the nostalgia of when we were young, how much time we had and how quickly the years are now going.

As the Dutch biologist, Midas Delckers, writes in *The Way of All Flesh: A Celebration of Decay* – 'your body is your museum to yourself'.

'Hawaii is hot and cold volcanoes, clear skies, and open ocean. Like most Pacific islands it is all edge, no centre, very shallow, very narrow, a set of green bowls turned upside down in the sea, the lips of the coastline surrounding the bulges of porous mountains.

This crockery is draped in a thickness of green so folded it is hidden and softened. Above the blazing beaches were the gorgeous green pleats of the mountains.'

    Paul Theroux 2001

Bali journal
August 2000

Hawaii – paradise in a traffic jam.

Things come in 3s. Firstly arriving in Paris and ringing Martine. Another cancer detection and back on chemo again. Then news of Xavier's father, Jean-Pierre, who ran the Washington Square Bar. A stroke some months back has forced him to close the bar. He can no longer play guitar and walks with a stick.

At the Royal Grove, I have known Joe for over 5 years. Retired and lived there for 10 years, always in the same chair in the lobby each morning saying hi to everyone. Well, not this year. He died at 90 some 5 months back after 12 months of illness. The girls have missed him but say he died where he was happy.

Long, long day from Paris to Honolulu. Two hours from Paris to Frankfurt, 1 hour wait. Nine and a half to Vancouver and 5 hours wait. Then 6 hour flight Vancouver to Honolulu. Nice to finally get to bed after 1.00am, to be woken by 2 backfires on the street below. Only that I find in the morning that they were gunshots. Another gun shot during the day following. 'Go stick your head around the corner and see if anyone is dead, Martin,' says Christie behind the front desk!

And the guy on the corner of the hotel who has been selling t-shirts there for 23 years. Now gutted out the shop for a sandwich bar with espresso machine. After 23 years! Hawaiians are like that. A small island, you can't go anywhere, except his children who now work in California.

Waikkiki 2016-10-26
Royal Grove Hotel, Hawaii
11 September 2002

16.12.11 On first flight out of Melbourne with our new airline 'Air Australia'. Lots of media hype, balloons, floral shirts at check-in. Free champagne on board served by attentive young things in what looked like refurbished Compass and Ansett clothing. Most cabin crew wearing shoes. All propellers appeared to be working. Landed on correct island. All for $200 one-way!

17.12.11 So good to be back at me favourite hotel, The Royal Grove – they considered becoming 5 Star, but then started having reservations ...

18.12.11 Hawaiian shirts and leis all at half mast and free open day at Pearl Harbour. And one-minute silence at new Trump Apartments, all to mourn 'the Donald' hairdo or to celebrate the death of Kim Jung Il (after long illness?). His son in line for new Korea move ...

19.12.11 Buy booze. Pay astronomical price for bottle of Gordons @ $A23. But then realize it's not 70ml, not 1 litre, but 1.75 litres. Experience similar feel to lottery win. These two ads on same catalogue page.

LIQUOR
COLLECTION
Honolulu's biggest little liquor store
Ward Warehouse

HAVE YOU EVER WISHED YOU
COULD SPEND ONE HOLIDAY
SOBER?
ALCOHOLICS ANONYMOUS
808-946-1438

21.12.11 Buy booze. Capitalise on the Champagne War pre Christmas. Moët at $34, Piper down to $29. Consider another 1.75 litre Gordons, but refrain as Barbara arriving. Forgot to go to Neil Sedaka concert, the rest of the world did too.

22.12.11 Advised by Donna at the desk that I may have to vacate my room – Barak, Michelle and the girls may ask for upgrade? Maybe a chance to move in with Barbara? Lots of security and road blocks in place, so not sure if for Barbara or the President.

24.12.11 It's beginning to smell a lot like Christmas. A bit like home in fact, but more oh! oh! oh! than ho! ho! ho!

Buy last minute booze in case of Christmas visitors.

25.12.11 Happy Christmas! Have superb dinner at Ocean House Restaurant with the lovely Donna, Barb and Aurora. A little bitching going on, but hey!, was Elvis this lucky with dates when here filming Blue Hawaii?

Aloha.

Extracts from Hawaii journal
December 2011

J

as in Jokes and Humour

Comedy is tragedy plus time.

Bad jokes found in Hawaii July 1999

- Why do blondes prefer cars with sunroofs? It gives them more legroom.
- What are the first words Japanese girls are taught? Gucci, Gucci, Gucci.
- I'm living in a tough neighbourhood – you can walk ten blocks without leaving the scene of the crime.
- Adam & Eve had the first computers – The Apple and the Wang.
- They're now testing athletes to see if they find any traces of sport.
- Does Spiderman have a website?
- Why do 24hr stores have locks on their doors?
- Asked the lawyer how much does it cost to answer two questions? '$5000, and what is the second question?'
- Local anaesthetics are for people who can't afford the imported kind.
- Just remember when you come second, you are the first of the losers.
- Cool people are scene and not herd.
- Suicide off a building – jumping to a conclusion.

US Journal 2004

This 'court document' (right) was compiled by myself and John Russo in his N.J. lawyers office. David had rung me early on a Sunday morning (July 2014) when I was staying at John's house.

Included here to celebrate David's life (1950 – 2007) and his infectious sense of humour. A true friend and best mate for many decades.

JOHN F. RUSSO , Esq.
307 FOREST GLEN AVENUE
FRANKLIN LAKES, NJ
P.O. BOX 161
RIDGEWOOD, NJ 07451-0161
(201) 251-7575
FAX (201) 891-5133
ATTORNEY FOR PLAINTIFF

Plaintiff	SUPREME COURT OF UNITED STATES CHANCERY DIVISION SOCIAL ETIQUETTE PART BERGEN COUNTY
MARTIN FOWLER	
vs.	Docket No. LT-55464-94
Defendant	Civil Action
	COMPLAINT
DAVE ATKINSON a.k.a. "Brave Dave"	

COUNT 1. I have been instructed by my client, Marty Fowler, to file a complaint & issue you a summons to prostrate yourself before the New York Court of Social Etiquette for an alleged violation & breach of the code of telephone usage, viz. causing a telephonic device to ring on Sunday 29 July in the year of the Lord 1994 at 8.15 a.m. New York time, shattering the quiet enjoyment & slumber being enjoyed at the Russo household, after the Plaintiff & writer had only several hours earlier returned from a night of social intercourse in the bars & cafes of New York city.

COUNT 2. The Plaintiff incorporates by reference each & every allegation of Count 1. as set out at length herein that the Plaintiff was a guest at the Russo household at the time the said telephone rang and when it became known to the Plaintiff & his hosts that the ignorant sot on the other end of the line was a friend & countryman, the Plaintiff suffered great shame, mortification & embarrassment at being associated with the Defendant. The Plaintiff sought & was treated for shock & emotional distress with coffee & bagels.   Wherefore the Plaintiff demands judgement-

1. By dissolving the long friendship between him & the Defendant.

2. That the Defendant be enjoined from ever telephoning the Plaintiff again.
3. That the Russo & the Fowler phone nos. be permanently erased from the Defendants teledex.
4. For compensatory & punitive damages based on the Defendants anti-social behavior.

Alternatively, this matter could be amicably resolved if the Defendant would present himself at the office of J.Russo & bring with him some suitable Australian liquid refreshment as an act of contrition for his objectionable conduct. The court also deputizes Sue Atkinson to take custody of the Defendant & deliver his body & bottle to the above referenced address to bear witness to his apology.

JOHN F. RUSSO-ATTORNEY FOR PLAINTIFF

Some good graffiti picked up along the way:
- Music students are cymbal minded
- Mathematicians always have a nice tan
- Geologists always find faults, but miners are more boring
- Old lawyers never die, they just lose their appeal
- Bo Peep did it for the insurance
- On condom vending machines –
  My father says they don't work
  Worst chewing gum I've tasted
  Cuts out oven doubt

〰〰

Flying Air New Zealand is different. Instead of the usual food service offering of 'Chicken or Beef?', comes a very sheepish 'Lamb or Lamb?'

Naturally, an interesting selection of wines accompany the meal; Lambrusco, a nice Shearaz and a Chateau Mutton-Rothschild ...

So, finish your food and wine, pull up the woollen blanket and enjoy a movie – Silence of the Lambs; Wolf Creek; Animal Kingdom; Sheepless in Seattle; Lambtana.

Melbourne to Honolulu 2009

K

as in knowledge

Genius is childhood
recovered at will.

Australia, 2001; The 'Clever Country' stumbles into 'Knowledge Nation'.

♒

Beware of all enterprises that require new clothes.
Henry David Thoreau

♒

One of the troubles of our age is that habits of thought cannot change as quickly as techniques, with the result that as skill increases, wisdom fades.
Bertrand Russell
Has Man a Future

♒

One of the tragic things I know about human nature is that all of us tend to put off living. We are all dreaming of some magical rose garden over the horizon, instead of enjoying the roses that are blooming outside our windows.
Dale Carnegie

♒

Most men make the voyage of life as if they carried sealed orders which they were not to open 'til they were fairly in mid-ocean.
JR Lowell

♒

If you don't take care of your mind and body, where else are you going to live?

Extract from 'In Search of Civilisation' by John Armstrong

2006

'... The key is that being civilised has more to do with what you are like, how you think and feel and act, rather than the big ideas to which you happen to be loyal.

A great idea can be believed fanatically, cruelly or superficially. The belief is fine but the believer isn't civilised.

You can fight for democracy and freedom, which are exceedingly good things, but do so in a way that is uncivilised.

You can go to the opera or art gallery, natural homes of civilisation, but just going there doesn't make you civilised. That depends on what happens to you there, how you engage, what you feel, and how that makes you – if it does – a finer person.

The simple fact is that there is no necessary connection between being loyal to something that is important to civilisation and being civilised ...

The central problem of civilised life – and civilisation – is in holding onto our ideals and putting them into workable versions, given the crooked timbers of humanity.

The awkward conjunction of pragmatism and idealism lies at the core of civilised life. Which is why we associate the word 'compromise' so readily with 'civilised'.

The essence of utopian fantasies is just this: the world would be perfect if people were different. And one might agree, but add: people are as they are, and you're not going to be able to do much about it …

The French poet Baudelaire once wrote a poem about an albatross. The huge bird soars magnificently in the empty skies but when brought down by an arrow onto the deck of a ship, it can hardly move its great bulk. It stands for the unworldly poet – intellectual; idealist becomes a fool, comic, tragic and useless, on the stage of ordinary life.

The opposite of the albatross is the 'weltkind' (child of the world), to steal a term from Goethe. The weltkind has an appetite for engaging with the world as it is, for facing the realities of authority, for getting on, for finding out how things work, for concrete success. Such a person isn't intimidated by the material world, or by the largely philistine powers that hold sway within it.'

Paris Journal 2006

Brown shoes don't make it.
Frank Zappa

How ridiculous and unrealistic is the man who is astonished at anything that happens in life.
Marcus Aurelius

Security is mostly superstition – avoiding danger is no safer in the long run than outright exposure. Life is either a daring adventure, or nothing.

    Writer Helen Keller

I don't know whether life has been a success or a failure. But not having any anxiety about becoming one instead of the other, and just taking things as they come along, I've had a lot of extra time to enjoy life.

    Harpo Marx

"There they were, sitting around the dinner table, knocking off a bottle of Côtes-du-Rhône and blathering about the Middle East—you've never heard such shallow, simplistic reasoning in your life—and one of them turns to me and says, 'And what do you think, Barney? What do you think we should do?' and all I could come up with was 'Woof.' I felt like such an ass."

« Ils étaient tous là à table, en train de siffler une bouteille de Côtes-du-Rhône, et de parler à tort et à travers du Moyen-Orient
– je n'avais jamais entendu un raisonnement aussi superficiel et simpliste de toute mon existence –
et puis l'un deux se tourne vers moi et me demande
« Que penses-tu de tout cela Barney ? Qu'est-ce qu'on doit faire ? »
Et tout ce que j'ai trouvé à dire c'était « Ouaff ! »
Je me suis senti vraiment con. »

L

as in Life

or having the ability to
play the hand you are
dealt.

It astonishes me how people waste their lives. The male life expectancy in Australia is about 600,000 hours: 200,000 sleep; 100,000 too young; 100 too old; 200,000 left. And most of that's spent washing the dishes, doing a boring job, dragging the dustbin down to the front gate. You're down to a very tiny pile of hours, probably 50,000 or 60,000. And most people fritter that away by looking at the tele or going to the footy. They look at ways to obliterate time, whereas I do lots and lots and lots of things, because life is short and I don't want to waste a minute.

Phillip Adams
1997

'*There were so many things now I would never fully understand, yet I was resigned to that, to my ignorance of the world. Life is too brief – since I first howled into the light, I have lived through changes that are merely the beginning of things I simply accept ...*'

    Found in Thea Astley's book The Multiple Effects of Rainshadow

    August journal, France 2000

And from the same book –

'*Je ne suis qu-un viveur lunaire*
Qui fait des ronds dans des bassins.'
(I am only a lunar reveller
Who makes circles in pools.)

~~~

'*We must not cry because it's over, but smile because it happened.*'
    Part of Adrian's obituary to his mother, my aunt Doris Walker.
    2005

I am sitting at a café on Seventh Avenue watching the world go by. My attention and focus dart to and fro – a girl in a red dress goes by, a man and a funny dog, the sun emerging from the clouds. These are all events which catch my attention for a moment as they happen. Why, out of a thousand possible perceptions, are these the ones I seize upon? Reflections, memories, associations lie behind them. For consciousness is always active and selective, charged with feelings and meanings uniquely our own, informing our choices and interfusing our perceptions. So it is not just Seventh Avenue that I see, but my Seventh Avenue, marked by my own selfhood and identity.

We are the directors of the film we are making – but we are, equally, its subjects too: every frame, every moment, is us, is ours – our forms are outlined in each one, even if we have no existence, no reality, other than this...

Finally then, we come around to Proust's image, that we consist entirely of 'a collection of moments', even though these flow into one another like Borges's river.

> Oliver Sacks, on The River of Consciousness
> Found in New York Review of Books
> January 2004

Loved this observation. A whole world is contained in those paragraphs.

Life itself is the proper binge.

    Chef, Julia Child

The only sin is mediocrity.

    Dancer, Martha Graham

There are dreams of love, life and adventure in all of us. But we are also sadly filled with reasons why we shouldn't try. These reasons seem to protect us, but in truth they imprison us. They hold life at a distance.

Life will be over sooner than we think. If we have bikes to ride and people to love, now is the time.

    Psychiatrist Elisabeth Kübler-Ross

What a wonderful life I've had! I only wish I'd realised it sooner.

    Writer, Colette

Life is the combination of magic and pasta, of fantasy and of reality.

    Federico Fellini

Many people will walk in and out of your life, but only true friends will leave footprints in your heart.
> Eleanor Roosevelt

*Great minds discuss ideas;
Average minds discuss events;
Small minds discuss people.*
> Eleanor Roosevelt

There are only two ways to live your life. One is as though nothing is a miracle. The other is as though everything is a miracle.
> Albert Einstein

Live as if you were already living for a second time and as if you had made the mistakes you are about to make now.
> Victor Frankl
> Physician, 90

If you wake up this morning with more health than illness, you're more blessed than the one million who will not survive this week.

If you have money in the bank or in your wallet or purse, you're among the top 8% of the world's wealthy.

So, work like you don't need the money – love like you've never been hurt – dance like nobody's watching – sing like nobody's listening – live like it's heaven on earth.
Found among correspondence from Perry Robinson
Paris 2002

*La vie ne vaut rien, mais
  Rien ne vaut la vie*
(Life is worth nothing,
but life means something)
> From Olivier Nebout
> Lyon 2001

I'm a success in one way. I started out with nothing and I still have most of it.

Diplomacy is the art of saying 'Good doggie', until you can find a rock.

A friend is a person who dislikes the same people you do.

If you help a friend in trouble he is bound to remember you – especially the next time he is in trouble.

'What can you know of life unless you have lived it? Everyone lives their life, one way or another, but we know what Maugham meant. My job has meant I often felt more like an observer than participant, eager to understand everyone's point of view but my own.

But I've lived my own life too, and hewn my novels out of its residue. I've known marriage, divorce, children, family, friends, neighbours, success, failure, hilarity, envy, astonishment, bewilderment, disappointment, grief, loss, the waxing and waning of love and of faith, the cold dawning of the truth about mortality, the sustaining warmth of constancy.

I've even lived through home renovations. Were it not for all that, I might be worried by the thought that, as a researcher, I had merely observed life from a window.'
    Hugh Mackay
    Social researcher
    The Age
    25 June 2005

Never explain yourself. Your friends don't need it and your enemies won't believe it anyway.

So, denial or acceptance? Most of us are living in quiet desperation; compulsive drinking helps.

M

as in music

'Music is the space
between the notes.'
– C. Debussy

J'ai deux amours –
Mon pays et Paris.
Paris toujours
C'est mon rêve joli

> verse from a song by Josephine Baker, 'J'ai Deux Amours'
>
> 1931

We didn't quite make it to America, but had a lot of fun rehearsing in Tony Hatter's Heidelberg garage, circa 1966.

Played at the IGS social and various other functions.

Claim to fame, winning 'Best Original Song', played at the 3UZ Battle of The Sounds, Festival Hall Melbourne.

≈

And I thought about years,
how they take so long
and they go so fast.
      from song of Beth Nielsen Chapman

The machine guns are roaring
And the puppets heave rocks,
And the fiends nail time bombs
To the hands of the clocks.

Call me any name I will never deny it
But farewell Angelina,
The sky is erupting,
I must go where it's quiet.

    from 60s Joan Baez song

*A*t best Asian music is off-brand American pop, like Sony Bono in a karaoke bar. At worst it sounds as if a truck full of wind chimes collided with a stack of empty oil drums during a birdcall contest.
    PJ O'Rourke

*M*usic students are cymbal minded.

*F*or I have seen children with faces much wiser than time.
    from Joan Baez song

Elvis impersonators still walk the earth, but if life were fair, Elvis would be alive and all the impersonators would be dead.
   Anon

~~~

Elvis fulfilled the terms of the contract. Excess, deterioration, self-destructiveness, grotesque behaviour, a physical bloating and a series of insults to the brain, self-delivered.
   Found in Don De Lillo's White Noise, 1985

~~~

Today is the anniversary of Elvis's death 20 years ago. Hawaii TV filled with it. CNN has 30 hour special covering all aspects – Elvis the Pelvis, GI Elvis, B Grade Movie Elvis, Bloated Elvis. Died-on-the-toilet Elvis.

There's the Complete Idiots Guide to Elvis book, the Elvis Cookbook. Questions and Answers on Elvis, e.g. Who built the Great Pyramids? Answer – Elvis.

Everything from a Finnish guy who has put down Elvis songs on a CD. In Latin. A singing dog named Elvis. It just went on.

His hair stylist was asked if Elvis had ever had a bad hair day. 'Without being disrespectful, it was on the day after his death when I had to go and do his hair at the funeral home.'

And his generosity was to be admired. There are 32 names on a plaque at the Memphis Caddy dealer. The last name is blank and they were all given a Caddy by Elvis. The un-named one was a man who Elvis saw at a bus stop. He looked like he was having a bad day, or more likely, a bad decade, so Elvis gave him a car.

Quote of the week though was 'People impersonate Elvis because it's too difficult to impersonate Bob Dylan.'

Hawaii journal
16.8.97

50 songs to listen to again before you lose your hearing:

1. House of the Rising Sun – Eric Burdon and the Animals
2. Angie – Rolling Stones
3. Behind Blue Eyes – The Who
4. Hotel California – The Eagles
5. Love – John Lennon
6. Sundown – Gordon Lightfoot
7. Stairway to Heaven – Pink Floyd
8. Thick as a Brick – Jethro Tull
9. Long May You Run – Neil Young
10. Blackbird – The Beatles
11. Walk on the Wild Side – Lou Reed
12. Skyline Pigeon – Elton John
13. Sky Pilot – Eric Burdon
14. Teach Your Children – Crosby, Stills and Nash
15. Lay Lady Lay – Bob Dylan
16. Georgia – Ray Charles
17. Are You Lonesome Tonight – Elvis Presley
18. Blue Bayou – Roy Orbison
19. Susanne – Leonard Cohen
20. Hallelujah – Leonard Cohen
21. If it be your will – Leonard Cohen, Webb sisters
22. Ain't No Sunshine – Bill Withers
23. The Letter – The Boxtops
24. Lady in Red – Chris deBurgh
25. City of New Orleans – Arlo Guthrie

26. Winter in America – Dough Ashdown
27. I'm Sorry – John Denver
28. Time in a Bottle – Jim Croce
29. Dock of the Bay – Otis Redding
30. There's not a cloud in the sky – Wendy Matthews
31. Girls in our Town – Margaret Roadknight
32. Six Ribbons – John English
33. You Were Always on my Mind – Willie Nelson
34. Over the Rainbow/Wonderful World – Israel Kamakawiwo'ole
35. Holding Back the Years – Simply Red
36. The Streets of London – Ralph McTell
37. Where do you go to – Peter Sarsted
38. Heard it Through the Grapevine – Creedence Clearwater Revival
39. It Don't Matter to Me – Bread
40. America – Simon and Garfunkle
41. Xanadu – Sarah Blasko
42. Fire and Rain – James Taylor
43. Without You – Harry Nilsson
44. If I was a Carpenter – Johnny Cash
45. God Only Knows – The Beach Boys
46. Seasons in the Sun – Terry Sacks
47. Going Back – Renee Geyer and Glenn Shorrock
48. Cool Change – Glenn Shorrock
49. Winds of Change – Scorpions
50. _____ – add your favourite!

N
as in New York

New York, New York – so good they charge you twice!

Hey, one hell of a town!

Manhattan is easy to get around. Streets run east-west, Avenues north-south. Fifth Ave is the dividing line between East and West.

The Villages highlight the ethnic and social mix that NY offers:

- Greenwich – extends west of Broadway from 14th St South to around Spring St.
- Chinatown – the area west of Chatham Square
- Soho – bounded by Broadway, Canal St, Avenue of the Americas and Houston St. Check out the cast iron buildings.
- Little Italy – Canal St North to Houston and from Elizabeth St West to Lafayette.
- Little India – around 6th St between 1st and 2nd Avenues.

So, a big, scary, dangerous city? Don't be fooled, it's just a village! But walk fast, talk faster – everything is 'gerrrd'.

It's in your face – it's a city where the main topic of conversation is your own city. Where people leave their curtains open of an evening and walk around naked if they want – they don't care, they are New Yorkers. And rituals are important to them. Saturdays, shopping – the impossible chic of Barneys, the elegant cool of Bergdorf Goodman, Saks Fifth Avenue. Then Central Park in the afternoon for lunch.

Sunday is brunch – all day. You are having pasta and a glass of white at 2.00pm and the couple next to you are having eggs easy over and French toast with the Sunday New York Times.

Ok, there are some pretty nice cities, but to be anywhere else at the moment would be irrelevant.

New York journal
July 1999

Even if you'd been waiting for the '90s ending crash throughout the '90s, even if you'd believed all along that further terrorism in New York was only a matter of when and not whether, what you felt on Tuesday morning wasn't intellectual satisfaction, or simply empathetic horror, but deep grief for the loss of daily life in prosperous, forgetful times.

 J. Franzen

 New Yorker, Sept 2001

... *And then September changed everything. If not the end of the year, then the end of the era; the end of certainty, the resumption of history ...*

 D. Macken

 Financial Review, December 2001

〰
〰

No pressures in New York? 'Look, take your time, just hurry.'

〰
〰

*I*t's one day away from the first anniversary of the moment that changed everything, but changed nothing.

Everybody is doing something. It has been strange to be travelling in both Canada and the US at this time and to see the reactions and attitudes.

Canada saw some 33,000 travellers diverted there when US airspace was closed. We didn't see in Australia the hardships and disruptions that that created and some moving stories were re-shown on the TV coverage today.

But the replayed footage of the four planes that crashed on that morning and the 3000 murdered, really hits home when you are here – Hawaii doesn't escape, as it has a strategic military base here.

Reflecting on all this was even more moving, at the battleship Arizona memorial at Pearl Harbour, the US's only other attack on its home soil – 1,177 sailors entombed underneath the floating shrine that you stand on.

As somebody said, you have to just try for a moment to put away all the other shit that is going on around in your head. Remember and think of the four planeloads of people who crashed into their deaths that morning and the thousands that they in turn killed.

Remember.

Thoughts on Nine-Eleven
Hawaii journal
2002

♒

*B*ack in New Jersey with John after many years. Two days in Manhattan, first in Lower area and second spent cycling in Central Park.

To think the Dutchman, Peter Minuit, paid $24 for Manhattan Island, now the Federal Bank stores a quarter of the world's gold bullion there!

There's a museum on every street, but no time – the place is a museum to itself. The gaping 20 acre hole at Ground Zero, with the rusted girder formed into a cross being the only remnant of the Twin Towers. Hard not to get tears in your eyes like so many others there – you can't describe the enormity of what happened. And the 300 kids who used to say 'My daddy's a fireman …'

And the Strand bookstore on Broadway. Established 1927 and now with 8 miles of books, some 2.5 million! Fantastic.

And up to the Dakota building on Amsterdam Ave, then across the street to Strawberry Fields to pay respects.

Afternoon tea at Tavern on the Green, watch the Dominican NY girl float across the floor for our order.

Drive back through Spanish Harlem – beaten-up cars, beaten-up women, piles of garbage, no English spoken and don't leave your car with the low-life you see on every corner.

U.S.A. journal
June 2004

♒

I'm in New York. I'm in New York and it's snowing ... Too overwhelmed to take notes, too busy to process it all. But this is my first time in the States and, to my surprise, I'm loving it.

Yes, I admit that I was apprehensive about coming here. America, I thought. That absurd and sometimes sinister place. Universe of the weird, cabaret of the kind of national solipsism that presses my scalp closer to my skull in unease. When I tell people here it's my first visit, they're amazed. To them it's the centre of the world.

But of course, I've been here all my life, I've seen it all so often. 5th Avenue, Lexington, Madison. Let's not forget Sesame Street. Maybe that's why I was wary of coming. America is so familiar to me from a thousand films, a hundred television shows, a shelf of novels. It's so well-represented on celluloid that I feel perhaps it's made of the stuff. Perhaps it doesn't really exist? I wondered if perhaps America was some kind of collective delusion, spun from hamburger wrappers, hairspray, Cadillacs, breast implants and parts of Brooklyn ...

Australians have been here before me, and I'm ridiculous in finding all this so amazing. I've been to famous cities before, I've trod boulevards that are mentioned in songs and lived in cities that gave rise to empires; it's not like I'm some hick. But being an ingénue in America, that's another thing. It's like entering not only a country but a cosmos ...

It's all so marvellous and cinematic and entertaining. I'm so tired: I don't know where I am anymore.
    24/02/07
    Kate Holden
    The Age

O

as in Oceans & Beaches

from Wye to Waimea,
all the world's a beach.

A beach observation from John Updike:

Here, the cinema of life is run backwards. The old are the first to arrive. They are idle, and have lost the gift of sleep. Each of our bodies is a clock that loses time ... The older we get and the fewer mornings left to us, the more deeply dawn stabs us awake.

*B*oneyard, Wongarra. Kent and I amongst the crowd. An exhilarating break with its long lines peeling across the shallow reef and kelp and up against the rocky shoreline. When you lose your board wish it well because, like your body when caught by these waves, it is practically bio-degradable.

The problem is not however the destruction by nature of expendable surfboards and human flesh, but the destruction by the crowds getting to these surf spots.

Yet, they are here with us, ten or so Mr. Universes sheathed in black neoprene, programmed to paddle at the first sign of a lineup appearing on the horizon.

We all jockey for position as the first wave rises on the reef. A couple of visitors sitting too far inside get caught and pay with ice cream headaches.

Number two in the set looks more impressive. Long strokes take most up over the face while a few paddle furiously and take off. The next one is bigger, maybe six? No more! Thicker and more hollow. And the noise! Like a freight train I yell to Kent. Nothing like this for months. My god you think, the noise; KG and I must be crazy to be out here. Heart pumping for the reason I moved to the coast. No time to paddle as she rises, pointing me to the dropping trough.

Feet skyward, I become a drawn arrow, fired across the glassy surface, waiting in a timeless void as her lip throws out over me for that long moment of a split second before I am devoured.

Wye River
May 1979

Come, my friends,
'Tis not too late to seek a newer world
Push off, and sitting well in order smite
The sounding furrows; for my purpose holds
To sail beyond the sunset, and the baths
of all the western stars, until I die.
It may be that the gulfs will wash us down:
It may be we shall touch the Happy Isles ...

    Poem Ulysses

    Tennyson

Bali journal 1993

I was fortunate to attend an epic surf contest at Huntington beach, California in July 1994.

By looking through the list below, it's not hard to see why the contest was dedicated to Tom Blake. He died at 92.

- 1922 Wins the 10 mile Open National Distance Swimming Championship
- 1924-64 Lifeguard and swimming instructor in Hawaii, California, Florida and New York
- 1926 Builds first hollow board
- 1930 Builds first waterproof camera housing
- 1931 Invents the sailboard
- 1935 Places the first fin on a surfboard
- 1966 Inducted into the International Surfing Hall of Fame
- 1971 Guinness Book of Records entry for longest surfboard ride on an ocean wave – 4,500 feet (1936)

We are riders – on the freeway, in our minds, everywhere and in every goddam aspect of our working lives. When push comes to shove and the job's screwed, kid's screaming, chequebook looks bleak, we must do only one thing. Paddle back out!
    Found in surf magazine

Bali 1996

Well, here it is nearing the end of the northern summer and after weeks of sun and beach in Hawaii, California and Vietnam I have a reasonable tan.

Yes I know you're not supposed to tan anymore. But hey, I love the sun and we all have to die of something so I figure you may as well look and feel good on the way out.

So, to hell with the Skin Cancer Police. Just enjoy those natural rays, slather on a cream with an SPF number close to your age and look better than you ever will when you go for your final lie down.

Vietnam journal
Hoi An beach
30.8.99

It's difficult to swim at many beaches now; you just go through the motions.

Life Around the Edges

It's been two months, thousands of kilometres and twenty-four beaches. All with a twenty-eight hundred dollar airfare.

Dividing the cost of the fare by the number of beaches, we come to an initial outlay of $116.60 per beach. As a study tour, I'm hoping to be able to claim at least most of this in taxation, together with a 'living away from home allowance'.

Here's a brief account:

1st leg – Hawaii
Beaches – Waimea, Three Tables, Sunset, Banzai, Waikiki, Turtle Bay, Ala Moana.

Where it all started. Mecca. Birthplace of Huey and where the ground trembles when the surf's big.

Only place where it's acceptable to go surfing in a stretch limo, where you can smoke cigars on the beach and wear 'the shirt'. Good Japanese food and saves you airfare to Japan. Elvis still lives here. Best bumper-sticker 'Drive It Like You Stole It'.

2nd leg – California
Beaches – Zuma, Malibu, Santa Monica, Venice, Long Beach, Huntington, Newport, Laguna, Corona del Mar, Santa Barbara, Jalama.

Like riding through a movie or TV show as the signs come up. Hollywood on the sand. Bob Dylan lives at Malibu, Neil Young at Jalama. More Porsches clog the carparks here than anywhere else. Best bumper-sticker on a Porsche – 'My Other Car's a Porsche'. Evidence everywhere of cosmetic surgery; surf in the morning, teeth-whitening in the afternoon. Other best bumper-sticker, 'I Surf The Real World'.

3rd leg – France

Beaches – Hendaye, Biarritz, Guéthary

So, maybe you haven't heard of them for surf, but seriously good beaches. Seriously crowded. Seriously, surfboards strapped to the top of the Renault? Best place not to be seen in a Hawaiian shirt. No cigars on the beach, but smog alert most days from cigarettes. This makes checking wave height difficult, but count on waves being similar in size to the cars. Topless women the norm, due to high price of French fashion. Bumper-stickers not chic and cars too small to wear one anyway. Le Big Mac! Evidence of red wine stains in sand.

4th leg – Bali

Beaches – Kuta, Legion, Seminyak, Canguu, Medowi

It doesn't come much better! Europe, America, Australia, Indonesia all rolled into one. McDonalds with the lot. If you're not on the beach in France in August, you're here. Legian is the visa checkpoint for Australians and Italians entering and departing Seminyak. More cafes and watch sellers than all the other beaches put together. Surfing under the protection of Mt Agung, Hawaii and the world's best come here when the North Shore is flat. Hawaiian shirt almost acceptable, but you'll be marked as gay. Few bumper-stickers, but better to tattoo one on your shoulder and walk around unnoticed.

So, until the next adventure, where there's water, there's life.

Bali journal
August 2000

Close your eyes. You're lying on the sand, face up to the warmth of the sun, towel drying fast in the heat from the dampness of your swimsuit – There's the sound of voices, distant, coming to you through your half-waking, half-sleeping dream – Boys, girls – The sound of their voices, and suddenly it seems you could be 13 again, 14, 15 – Lying near-naked on the sand and aware of yourself in a way you've never been before – stretched out there for all the world to see and just waiting for those voices to get nearer and nearer, for a shadow to fall over your face so you open your eyes and some boy you like is standing over you, or some girl looking you up and down.

Something about the beach does this to you, I think, turns you into a teenager again. Doesn't matter how many times you trawl off with the tartan blankets and the children and the chilly bin, when you flop down at last, strip down to your swimsuit and rub a bit of suntan cream onto your shoulders – Bang. You're right back there in the midst of one of those rites-of-passage moments from adolescence. Suddenly it's just you and your body and the bodies of others. That's all that counts. Nothing else to think about for now except the flatness of your belly, the colour of your skin as it bakes in the heat ...

For where else but a place like the great Australian beach do you get to see quite as many bodies, quite so close up? Where else in life do people get to present themselves to each other in quite the same way? ...

With the sun overhead and the blue sea glittering at your back, it's like all the lights are turned on bright, like the curtain has been raised and this is the most brightly lit stage of all. For this is the time when the drama of adulthood starts, for many of us – the time when we leave childhood behind and move onto the stage of adult life. No wonder photographers find the beach irresistible ...

... It is the sense of the physical: the way the beach highlights that particular sense of ourselves as a combination of nothing more than skin and hair and flesh and bone. Just as we feel our bodies acutely on the beach – are we too hot? Do we need a swim yet? Is this towel I'm lying on too wet? Is my head comfortable resting on the sand? – just as we notice our bodies, our skin, as we pick the sand off that bit behind our knees and rub oil into our bellies, so we become reduced somehow to that singular, physical vision of ourselves ...

Maybe that's why the drama of age and youth is played out so dramatically. Because there are no other factors in this contest on the sand other than sheer physical performance ...

The beach drama captures all that sense of boys and girls together, the teasing, the uncertainties, with all of the bravado of showing off and playing up – but it explores the vulnerability of adolescence, too. The teenager we see on the beach is actually a part of us still: the person who doesn't quite know what to say, doesn't quite know the right thing to do. That's interesting, to me, that not-knowing, that not-quite-being.

It's interesting to remember the kids we were, the kids we still are, to some extent, inside.

>   Life Laid Bare
>   Part of an essay by Kirsty Gunn
>   The Age 13.1.07

P

as in Poetry

'What a heavy thing is
a pen!'
– Emile Zola

Good morning Mrs. Roebuck;
Hello Mr. Blighty.
Good morning Mrs. Simpson,
Jesus Christ almighty.

BREAKING THE APRON STRINGS

WHEN my grandmother died
I had to kiss her three times
(I was scared)
My mother said
Do not fear death
It is only the last stranger
You meet in life.
When I was 13
My mother kissed me
Three times
(I thought I was going to die)
My mother said
Now, my child, you must carry
Your own sins.

  L.E. SCOTT

There was a little girl,
Who had a little curl
Right in the middle of her forehead.
When she was good
She was very, very good
And when she was bad
She was diagnosed with Attention Deficit Hyperactivity Disorder.

WHAT IS NOT GENERALLY KNOWN

This is not generally known. Some time ago
(about the time when the first star got ready to twinkle and
flicker)
it became a good idea for fish to try and walk. Well it was roughly
that time. Anyway.
Soon the fish became monkeys
though for one thing I'm certainly not sure how.
Some say a big flood followed. Others refute this suggestion
(I think it's a question of how you wear your hair). But to
continue.
It's all just a hop skip and a jump from there.
We finally lost our tails, some thinker thought
it might be nice
to make god (and after that lots of people
tended to kill
lots of other people, depending on the homeground
advantage),
cows were discovered to be tasty, numbers and infinity
both vogue philosophies, electricity was a thing
we brought
out of the sky, and there was good stuff
found beneath us.

If only those trees weren't in the way ('hey
lets use the trees'
some bright spark thought). Money became
the new god
which all ex-fish worshipped. Only, not many
found their succour.
Small men in suits ran about everywhere in a vague attempt
at control. All sorts of other stuff happened.
The moon
was walked on. Telephony got to be the
new telepathy.
Out there, the universe continued to expand.
Cities did here.
No Martian was officially recorded landing.
Not any old god.
Answers became products. Everything got
discovered
and sold. Listen; they're talking about
building machines
that think now. Another thing generally
not known is that
very little of this actually matters greatly at all.
    DAN DISNEY

Sunlight breaks.
Not the strings of kites
But the haze and morning smoke
of cooking fire and crackling clove.
The morning of the world awakes.

With eyes that speak what
No lips can impart,
Ibu, with flower in outstretched hand
Approaches proud with breast bare
And child curved to her side —
A jigsaw piece waiting to be
removed from the puzzle

  M.F

Two poems written
on moving into Taman Sari Cottages, Bali
June 1988

Sound, sound the clarion, fill the fife,
Throughout the sensual world proclaim,
One crowded hour of glorious life
Is worth an age without a name
      T. MORDAUNT
      1729-1809

AUSTRAL ENDS

1. This is a land without Predators
   The world Down Under
   The stange material of a different soil
   Lost between ice and equator.

2. It is a mystery of another universe
   Dead and living trees
   Primordial bush
   Pierced by the grey lightning
   of the marsupial leap.
   It is a forest billy of hot eucalypt smell
   From which the germinal incense rises
   Where the white man has not been.

3. It is a land whose valleys
   are dreamt of by the rainbow-snake
   Where red dust is imprinted
   by the honey-ant
   Where humans – last guests
   invited to this principal feast –
   seem mute of gesture
   In this time non-existent.

4. It is a wonderful palette of surreal animals
   Possum, emu and platypus
   Wallaby, wombat and koala
   Half reptile, half mammal
   And even a devil
   From the mighty depth of Tasmania.

5. But the Lyre-bird can sing better than me
   this unique Bestial world
   Rests nowhere else
   After the Great Noah's Ark.

6. It is a roll of crashing waves
   on a sandy body curved
   between the wind and immensity
   A whole ocean of broken foam
   From where suddenly
   springs the angry light of the shark's eye

7. It is a music score of Blue Mountains
   Preserved by the gnawing centuries
   Punctuated by happy streams
   Whose cliffs conserve as treasure
   coming to us through millions of years
   Thirty tall pine trees
   The rough trunks
   of which knew the rub of the dinosaurs

8. It is a waltz of multicolour fish
   collecting the coral in the brightness
   the pure instant when the soul faints
   Overflowed by the wave of happiness

9. The world Down Under
   is a land without predators
   The strange matrixof a different soil
   And in this Austral beautiful land
   With a wild taste of origin
   My travelling heart fell in love.

   Thierry Cozon

   (translated from the French T.C + M.F January 2001)

Plea from a lobby of marginalised,
oppressed, disempowered,
disenfranchised and persecuted tuna.

I am not sleek and intelligent
like a dolphin,
nor have their constant grin.
I am not cute and furry
like a harp seal.
Lack the size of a whale or elephant.
I am not high up the chain of being
like an orangutan.
I'm lost in great schools
without the charm of identity.
OK I am cold blooded
like a snake
& even vegetarians
find little harm done eating me
but my mother
(since netted, gaffed & canned)
loved me
& always told me that I
was just as good
as any son-of-a-bitch mammal.

   ROLAND LEACH

Sand
sand
mountains
slowly turned
beaten by the sea
by the wind
falls through my fingers
presses tight in my fist.

Soft bed for the dead man
for the lovers
who ever dream long sighing
that the sand
falling grain upon grain
in the hour glass
where one hour is measured
by a million
upon million years

  JOHN ROOKE

They're still hurling rocks in
The East,
Now some fall on Paris
And some on Nice.
But cloak, veil and scarf
Can't mask the case that
The West has never concealed
The face except of course
of the executioner.
    MF
    Paris 2016

The singer Mouloudji was born in Paris in 1932. He gave a summary of a few of the things that made him French:

Catholic by my mother
Moslem by my father
A little Jewish by my son
Buddhist on principle

Alcoholic by my uncle
Neurotic by my grandmother
Classless by long-felt shame
Depraved by my grandfather

Royalist by my mother
Fatalist by my brother
Communist by my father
Marxist by imitation

Double-dealing like a lawyer
Sensual like a miser
Tough like a soldier
Gentle like a drunkard

Deceived by my better half
Pestered by my concierge
Hated by my neighbours
Detested by dogs

Athiest, o thanks to God
Athiest, o thanks to God.

The Surfer

He thrust his joy against the weight of the sea;
climbed through, slid under those long banks of foam –
(hawthorn hedges in spring, thorns in the face of stinging).
How his brown strength drove through the hollow and coil
of green – through the weirs of water.
Muscle of arm thrust down long muscle of water;
and swimming so, went out of sight
where mortal, masterful, frail, the gulls went wheeling
in air as ho in water, with delight.

Turn home, the sun goes down; swimmer, turn home.
Last leaf of gold vanishes from the sea-curve.
Take the big roller's shoulder, speed and swerve;
come to the long beach home like a gull diving.

For on the sand the grey-wolf sea lies snarling,
cold twilight wind splits the waves hair and shows
the bones they worry in their wolf-teeth. O, wind blows
and sea crouches on sand, fawning and mouthing;
drops there and snatches again, drops and again snatches
its broken toys, its whitened pebbles and shells.

    Judith Wright

    c. 1945

If you can keep your head when all about you
    Are losing theirs and blaming it on you;
If you can trust yourself when all men doubt you,
    But make allowance for their doubting too;
If you can wait and not be tired by waiting,
    Or being lied about, don't deal in lies,
Or being hated don't give way to hating,
    And yet don't look too good, nor talk too wise:

If you can dream—and not make dreams your master;
    If you can think—and not make thoughts your aim;
If you can meet with Triumph and Disaster
    And treat those two impostors just the same;
If you can bear to hear the truth you've spoken
    Twisted by knaves to make a trap for fools,
Or watch the things you gave your life to, broken,
    And stoop and build 'em up with worn-out tools:

If you can make one heap of all your winnings
    And risk it on one turn of pitch-and-toss,
And lose, and start again at your beginnings
    And never breathe a word about your loss;
If you can force your heart and nerve and sinew
    To serve your turn long after they are gone,
And so hold on when there is nothing in you
    Except the Will which says to them: 'Hold on!'

If you can talk with crowds and keep your virtue,
    Or walk with Kings—nor lose the common touch,
If neither foes nor loving friends can hurt you,
    If all men count with you, but none too much;
If you can fill the unforgiving minute
    With sixty seconds' worth of distance run,
Yours is the Earth and everything that's in it,
    And—which is more—you'll be a Man, my son.

Rudyard Kipling

Ozymandias

I met a traveller from an antique land
Who said: Two vast and trunkless legs of stone
Stand in the desert … Near them, on the sand,
Half sunk, a shattered visage lies, whose frown,
And wrinkled lip, and sneer of cold command,
Tell that its sculptor well those passions read
Which yet survive, stamped on these lifeless things,
The hand that mocked them, and the heart that fed:
And on the pedestal these words appear:
'My name is Ozymandias, king of kings:
Look on my works, ye Mighty, and despair!'
Nothing beside remains. Round the decay
Of that colossal wreck, boundless and bare
The lone and level sands stretch far away.

   Percy Bysshe Shelley

Sensuality

Feeling hunger and cold, feeling
Food, feeling fire, feeling
Pity and pain, tasting
Time in a kiss, tasting
Anger and tears, touching
Eyelids with lips, touching
Plague, touching flesh, knowing
Blood in the mouth, knowing
Laughter like flame, holding
Pickaxe and pen, holding
Death in the hand, hearing
Boilers and bells. Hearing
Birds, hearing hail, smelling
Cedar and sweat. Smelling
Petrol and sea, feeling
Hunger and cold, feeling
Food, feeling fire ....
Feeling

     Kenneth Slessor

Crossing the Bar

Sunset and evening stars,
And one clear call for me!
And may there be no moaning of the bar,
When I put out to sea,

But such a tide as moving seems asleep,
Too full for sound and foam,
When that which drew from out the boundless deep
Turns again home.

Twilight and evening bell,
And after that the dark!
And may there be no sadness of farewell;
When I embark;

For tho' from out our bourne of Time and Place
The flood may bear me far,
I hope to see my pilot face to face
When I have crossed the bar.
    Alfred, Lord Tennyson

Grief fills the room up of my absent child,
Lies in his bed, walks up and down with me,
Puts on his pretty looks, repeats his words,
Remembers me of all his gracious parts,
Stuffs out his vacant garments with his form.
    Shakespeare,
    From King John

The Last Days of Chrome (For my XP Falcon)

This car has seen a lot of hats
remembers shillings and pence
miles per gallon
It was here before McDonald's
before garlic and miniskirts
It drove through Woodstock
This car has known love
One owner and the same mechanic
for 25 years
One took her places
the other got inside her
touched her heart
kept it singing
the sweet song of engine joy
This car has been polished, chamoised
stroked like a magic lantern –
climb in and arrive somewhere else
This car looks like something
in an old National Geographic
Dull gold, bright silveroriginal heavy metal
trailing a throaty exhaust
like a movie queen's backward glance
The ancestors of the tail-lights
are science fiction rockets
The dashboard's still on its way to
Mars
This car is a living messenger
from the last days of chrome
when motoring was an act of beauty
when cars had mouths and ate the air
above empty, perfect roads.

      Lauren Williams

Q

as in quotes, puns, thoughts & chiasmus

read, learn and care; you may grow in the process.

I never travel without my diary. One should always have something sensational to read on the train.
   Oscar Wilde.

Il y a ceux qui marchant sous la pluie et ceux qui se font moviller.

There are those who walk in the rain and there are those who get wet.

Found in Paris, July 2008

The whole aim of practical politics is to keep the populace alarmed (and hence clamorous to be led to safety) by menacing it with an endless series of hobgoblins, all of them imaginary.
   H.L. Mencken
   American author and social critic
   (1880-1956)

'There is more history in a piece of cheese than a museum'.

∼∼∼

*W*ish I hadn't read that twenty years ago because it somewhat framed my itineraries.

They say to understand a city you must have had time to waste in it. I'm extremely guilty of this; generally no agenda, no list of tourist must-sees and now, for over a decade, another 'No museums, no temples-cathedrals' trip. OK, I'll visit the Louvre and the D'Orsay once more, but look at these as galleries as justification.

Sure, many of the world's natural attractions, great cities and monuments are worth seeing. But as Samuel Johnson said 100 years ago;

'Worth seeing? Yes. but not worth going to see.'

I'll concur too with the enigmatic exile, traveller, writer and remittance man, Paul Bowles (1910-1999), that if faced with the decision of choosing between a cathedral, café and public monument, or a fiesta and a museum, he would take the café and the fiesta.

On TGV
Paris to Grenoble
8/8/11

〰️

- Light travels faster than sound. This is why some people appear bright until you hear them speak.
- Scientists say that the universe is made up of Protons, Neutrons and Electrons. They forgot to mention Morons.
- Artificial intelligence is no match for natural stupidity.
- Alzheimer's can't be that bad. You get to meet new people every day.
- And the worst part of surviving a plane crash in the wilderness. Your biggest concern would be how much your airport parking was going to be.
- Instead of 'shithole' countries, surely it would have been more polite for Trump to say 'Turd World'?

〰️

To the eternal triple question which has always remained unanswered, who are we? Where do we come from? and Where are we going? I reply:

As far as I, personally, am concerned, I am me; I come from just down the road; and I am now going home.

    Pierre Dac,

    popular French comedian

    found in Paris, August 2007

Printed on bottom of Henry Miller's stationery –

cuando merda tiver valor pobre nasce sem cu
(when shit becomes valuable, the poor will be born without arseholes)

〜〜

Australia: I like the way we've been able to fuck things here as good as anywhere else in only half the time.
    epigram by LAURIE DUGGAN
    in The Oxford Book of Modern Australian Verse

〜〜

5% of people make things happen

15% watch it happen

80% wonder what's happened

〜〜

The really compassionate course would be to turn off the life support system and put us out of our misery

〜〜

If less is more, does a little bit more mean you end up with a little bit less?

The difference between a rut and a grave is the depth.
    G. BURRILL

〜〜

The world is a tragedy for those who feel and a comedy for those who think.

Salesmen are people who enter revolving doors behind you but come out in front.

Politicians are people who shake the hands of half the people in the room and the confidence of the rest.

Wilderness should exist intact for its own sake – no justification, rationale or excuse is needed. For its own sake and no other reason.

〜〜

You are never too old to have a happy childhood.
    found on the back of an RV van in Canada
    by Jenny & Peter Erlanger, 1993

〜〜

Mirrors would do well to reflect a little more before sending back images.
    J. COCTEAU

Vietnam journal
September 1999

Found articles on Chiasmus. Defined as a reversal in the order of words in two otherwise parallel phrases. An American, Dr. M. Grothe has devoted a web site to this (www.chiasmus.com).

Churchill, Kennedy, Wilde and Shaw were masters of chiasmus. A.J. Liebling wrote of himself in The New Yorker, 'I can write better than anybody who can write faster, and I can write faster than anybody who can write better.'

Double chiasmus comes in this example from Leonardo da Vinci, 'Painting is poetry that is seen rather than felt, and poetry is painting that is felt rather than seen.'

And there is implied chiasmus, in which you have to imagine the first unspoken part of the coupled phrases, eg. Mae West's famous 'a hard man is good to find' and Kermit's 'time's fun when you're having flies'.

~~~
~~~

Paris. The world comes and goes every day; some stay, some just visiting or passing through. Everything changes but everything is still the same. Does it really matter where Hemmingway took his coffee, which artists lived and painted on the hill of Montmartre, or where Gertrude Stein lived, or who or when someone was buried at Cemetery Père Lachaise? No more really than where you take your coffee that morning. It's just knowing that Paris was there for them as it is there for you.

Paris Journal

2009

The most entertaining surface on earth is the human face.
G. LICHTENBERG

I grew up in Bali; I grew old in Paris

To travel well.

To travel well, you have to be optimistic and energetic, not easily discouraged or inclined to depression. But not too sentimental either. And to realise that if something can go wrong, it usually might.

Vietnam diary
2016

Reply by L.B Johnson to reporter –

'Why are you asking me all these chicken shit questions?'

R

as in Religion

'If you want to make God laugh, tell him your plans for life.'
– Woody Allen

*H*aving had a lot of travel time in Christian, Buddhist, Hindu and Muslim countries, it's been impossible to categorize the best, the worst, or the most appropriate religion to live by. It's been so much easier and simpler to live without one.

With travel, it becomes obvious that no one religion is any better or different than another. So many religions and gods to believe in, but no rational argument or reason to follow any of them.

Religion has continually distorted the world, from The Inquisition right through to the Islamic extremism we witness today. Bertrand Russell noted in 1927, yes 1927, that the more intense and dogmatic a religion in any period, the greater was the cruelty inflicted on the society of that time.

Most people also tend to have followed the religion they were taught in infancy. They have adopted the predominant beliefs of their family and community, rather than for any intellectual reason.

So, the notion that one religion is better than another, or more true, becomes painfully silly. Yes, they can all be movingly beautiful and a lovely flight from reality, but at the same time be quite absurd. Just as with agriculture, electricity and science, I see religion as a man made invention.

Having clinically died a couple of times during cardiac arrest in 2012, there was certainly nothing 'out there' that I can report on. Or any encouragement to have stayed on for a possible better after-life.

James Leuba, the now departed American psychologist stated that the true religious believer dies in a gang, like a soldier. He escapes the paralysing sense of aloneness which must inevitably overtake the sceptic in the end.

I hope to experience that aloneness too, the next time around.

Lorne, 2015

"This time of year, with the office parties and the family visits, and having to shop for everyone you know—I'm truly thankful that I'm inside."

'On entering adult life, however, a young person so educated (with taboos on sex knowledge) will find himself or herself plunged into a world full of injustice, full of cruelty, full of preventable misery. The injustice, the misery, and the cruelty that exist in the modern world are an inheritance from the past, and their ultimate source is economic, since life and death competition for the means of subsistence was in former days inevitable. It is not inevitable in our age.

'With our present industrial technique we can, if we choose, provide a tolerable subsistence for everybody. We could also secure that the world's population should be stationary if we were not prevented by the political influence of Churches which prefer war, pestilence and famine to contraception.

'The knowledge exists by which universal happiness can be secured; the chief obstacle to its utilization for that purpose is the teaching of religion. Religion prevents our children from having a rational education; religion prevents us from removing the fundamental causes of war; religion prevents us from teaching the ethic of scientific co-operation in place of the old fierce doctrines of sin and punishment.

'It is possible that mankind is on the threshold of a golden age; but, if so, it will be necessary first to slay the dragon that guards the door, and this dragon is religion.'

> Found in 'Has Religion Made Useful Contributions to Civilization?'
> Bertrand Russell
> Why I Am Not a Christian
> (Touchstone, 1967)

If history were to repeat ...?

DA VINCI · PL. 7

THE LAST SUPPER
[DETAIL]

'The truly civilized man, it seems to me, has already got away from the old puerile demand for a 'meaning in life'. It needs no esoteric significance to be interesting to him. His satisfactions come, not out of a childish confidence that some vague and gaseous god, hidden away in some impossible sky, made him for a lofty purpose and will preserve him to fulfil it, but out of a delight in the operations of the universe about him and of his own mind, regardless of the way it takes him, just as it delights the lower animals, including those of his own species, to exercise their muscles.

'If he really differs qualitatively from those lower animals, as all theologians agree, then that is the proof of it. It is not a soul that he has acquired; it is a way of thinking, a way of looking at the universe, a way of facing the impenetrable dark that must engulf him in the end, as it engulfs the birds of the air and the protozoan in the sea ooze.

'Thus he faces death, the inexorable – not, perhaps, with complete serenity, but at least with dignity, calm, a gallant spirit. If he has not proved positively that religion is not true, then he has at least proved that it is not necessary. Men may live decently without it and they may die courageously without it. But not, of course, all men...'

> found in Treatise On The Gods, (John Hopkins University Press, 2006)
> by H.L. MENKEN (1880-1956)

My alternative Ten Commandments,

                      devised on the plane to New York,
                                           September 2000.

1. The greatest risk is not taking one.
2. The only sin is mediocrity.
3. Avoid the devastatingly dull.
4. Win at the slowest possible speed.
5. Don't come second; you're the first of the losers.
6. Beware of all enterprises that require new clothes.
7. Don't snooze or you lose.
8. It's your future – be there.
9. Trust everyone, just make sure you get to shuffle the cards.
10. Die young at an advanced age.

In the beginning, God created the earth and then rested.
Then God created Man and rested.
Then God created Woman.
Since then, neither God nor Man has rested.

      from Perry Robinson, 2003.

Found in P.J. O'Rourke's 'Modern Manners'
(Atlantic Monthly Press, 1994)

Some traditional social events are still very much with us even though everybody wishes they weren't.

This goes double for Christmas ...

There is a remarkable breakdown of taste and intelligence at Christmas time. Mature, responsible, grown men wear neckties made out of holly leaves and drink alcoholic beverages with raw egg yokes and cottage cheese in them. Otherwise reasonable adult women start hinting about emerald bracelets before they even get their brassieres off ...

The worst part of Christmas is dinner with the family, when you realize how truly mutated and crippled is the gene stock from which you sprang ...

It's customarily said that Christmas is done 'for the kids'. Considering how awful Christmas is and how little our society likes children, this must be true.

Bali journal,
September 2001

... Good and evil, God and the infidel, each have been at each other's throats throughout history. Witness the 150 years of the Crusades from 1095. The Christians travelled to the other side of the known world to cut the enemy's throats and claim the kingdom of God back from the Muslims. Europe has been the bloodsoaked battleground for beliefs from all parts of the compass, based on empire, religion, greed, power and sheer vengeance.

Through all this, the Great Satan has taken many forms, and being of 'ex silentio' nature, easily adaptable to whatever cause suits. Exhortations and denunciations, all the better to be omnipresent because the danger is always 'clear and present'. The Great Satan has materialised most recently as the US, whose policies towards the Middle East are regarded by many militant groups as the route of all their misfortune ...

Because of the internet, murder has entered our lives quicker than ever before. What other generation has seen in their living rooms the moments before a man or woman, drained of hope, a life bereft of future, on their knees, knowing death stands behind them? We have seen it, more than once, and once was enough ...

The difference with latter-day terrorists is that they do not seek transformation of their targets. A target is not a lump of clay to be moulded into the same image as the sculptor. A target is there simply to be hurt.

It is nihilism wrapped in hatred that has made the term 'clear and present danger' a weapon in itself. Critics of the US Patriot Act and the increased powers given to security agencies in Britain and Australia say civil liberties are being sacrificed on the altar of this nebulous justification.

Islamic hardliners bear the brunt of this attention, but are their utterances a constituent of clear and present danger to the society in which we live? It's a line of casualty nigh impossible to prove beyond reasonable doubt.

And we are a reasonable society, are we not?

   extract from article, Age Review 24.9.05
   Warwick McFadyen

Some Jewish jokes, picked up along the way –

- Why do Jewish husbands die early?
  Because they want to.
- Why don't Jewish mothers drink?
  It interferes with their suffering.
- What do Jewish women make for dinner?
  Reservations.
- There is a big controversy on the Jewish view of when life begins; in Jewish tradition, the foetus is not considered viable until it graduates from medical school.
- Short summary of every Jewish holiday: They tried to kill us, we won, let's eat.
- A Jewish boy gets a part in the school play. 'Wonderful, what part is it?' says the mother. The boy says, 'I get to play the part of the Jewish husband.' The mother scowls and says 'Go back and tell the teacher you want a speaking part.'
- A Jewish grandmother is watching her grandchild playing on the beach when a huge wave comes and takes him out to sea. She pleads 'Please God, save my only grandson I beg of you, bring him back.' And a big wave comes and washes the boy back on the beach, safe and well. She looks up to heaven and says 'But he had a hat.'

≈

I liked the musings of philosopoher George Satayana to the effect that in the flood of life, it is futile and unnecessary to seek spiritual design and harmony where none is to be found.

France Journal
2015

Courage to Care

First of all, I would like the thank the Organisers of the Courage to Care Exhibition for inviting me to tell my story during the Holocaust and shortly afterwards.

I was 7 ½ years old when, on the 19th March 1944, the German Occupying Forces moved in to Hungary. Eichmann was put in charge of what the Nazis called 'The Final Solution' – that is, the complete eradication of the Jewish population of Europe.

It is now 64 years ago, and as a result of this, my memory may not be exact, but it is very deep inside me, even after all these years.

Having come from a traditional Jewish family, living in Budapest, this naturally affected me very deeply. At the time, I thought that is was just a big adventure – seeing military hardware, foreign uniforms and war planes.

Up until that day, I felt secure, attended the local primary school and I had not felt any discrimination – but I would like to stress once again that I was only 7 ½ years old. This soon changed. As a Jew, I could no longer attend school – which, at the time, I thought was great, and I did not go to school for another 12 months.

New rules and regulations were of a daily occurrence from here on. We had to wear a distinguishing Yellow Star on our clothes over our heart – approximately 10 centimetres across and also a curfew was placed on us as to when we could go into the streets.

Nazi officials came to each building and they collected all valuables in the name of the 'War Effort'. Very carefully they made lists of everything we handed in, valued all items, gave us receipts and of course we have never seen them again. My greatest loss was our radio. Up until that time we could follow the events of the war – very biased, but nevertheless I could use my atlas to see where the fighting was.

Soon, all males over the age of 16 were called up. This included my father, 11 uncles and 4 cousins – the oldest was about 50 years of age. Of these 16 people, only 2 were alive 12 months later.

In the streets, anybody wearing the Yellow Star was fair game. People were rounded up at random. They disappeared and their fate was only made clear at the end of the war.

The next set of regulations created what they called 'designated houses'. These became the only houses where Jews could live. The block of flats where we lived had 30 apartments – approximately ½ of which were occupied by Jewish tenants, and our house was one of these 'designated houses', probably because of the large proportion of existing Jewish tenants. So, into our tiny 2-room apartment, 3 aunts and 3 female cousins joined us.

Food was getting scarce, it was rationed and the Jewish population could only get approximately ½ of the normal rations.

My father was in a Forced Labour camp from April 1944 to July 1944. At the time, he came home for 1 night with the news that his Unit will be moving the following day. I still remember him saying that there is one thing they will never be able to take away from you, and that is education. That was the last time I saw my father. He died in Germany in a Concentration Camp.

In July 1944, Raoul Wallenburg arrived in Budapest. I will get back to him shortly. His mission was to rescue the remaining Hungarian Jews from certain death. He issued 'Protective Passes' to help save some people. My family managed to get one for my father, but sadly, either it did not reach him, or if it did, then it did not help him.

During all this time, we were also bombed very regularly by the Allies – the British were more accurate than the Americans. Constant air raids kept us nearly as much in the cellars as in out apartments. I was very scared of the bombings. The whistle of the bomb and the noise of the explosions were very frightening. Buildings collapsed, incendiary bombs burnt houses down and death and injuries became common place and some were horrendous. Sometimes I saw aeroplane dogfights and through some gaps in the brick work I even managed to see the odd aeroplane being shot down. Somehow, I felt that the closer the fighting was, the closer the end may be.

Our bags were always packed – we were prepared for either air raids or for deportation and we could only put the most essential items in a small bag.

We lived in this relative 'calm' until October 1944.

At that time a new wave of terror started when the Hungarian Nazi Arrow Cross Party took over the power. As there were no more trains in working order, they deported the women and children on a 'Death March' towards the Austrian border. At this stage all my family were deported except for myself

It was at this time, that I had my very first encounter with people who had COURAGE TO CARE. They were our immediate next door neighbours, living in an adjoining apartment. They were

Christians, took me in, hid me in their apartment in a small room, and I was not to move from this room for about 6 weeks. I could not even go to the cellar during air raids for fear of being recognised. This would have meant instant death not only to myself, but to Mrs. Molnar and her 2 daughters, who were hiding me. The family have also shared their meagre food supply with me.

I wonder how many of us, today, would risk our own lives, just to hide somebody!

From their point of view, it was just natural. This family was just some of the many unheralded Righteous Gentiles.

My mother and aunts who were on this 'Death March' to the Austro-Hungarian border were rescued and brought back to Budapest by Raoul Wallenburg's rescue mission. They managed to get false Identity papers – officially as 'refugees from the advancing Soviet Army' and I joined them in hiding. However, as I was the only male amongst them. I was regarded as a risk factor, as only Jewish males were circumcised at that time in Hungary and recognition would not have been difficult.

So, it was decided that I should go to one of the Swedish Red Cross children's shelters. On my first attempt, I did not succeed in getting there, as there was an air raid on my way to this shelter. On the following day I returned once again as there was an Identification road block, and it would have been too dangerous for me. On the 3rd day, when I got to the shelter, I found it empty, so I returned home. I found out later, that the children were all taken away from there by the Arrow Cross the night before, and every second child was shot in to the River Danube. The others were tied to the ones they shot and thus they were to drown in the freezing river.

Death was all around us constantly, and I became quite immune to bodies and the smell of decomposing flesh.

Between Christmas 1944 and mid-January 1945 we were constantly in the cellars, We had no food whatsoever during this fortnight and I had only a dozen sugar cubes to eat, which my mother managed to steal from somebody. We had no problems regarding water, as there was plenty of snow outside. The noise of the bullets and artillery fire was deafening and very frightening.

One day there was an unusual calm for about an hour and suddenly, we noticed that the soldiers were wearing a different uniform. They were the Russian liberating troops and they brought us our first meal in 2 weeks – the best tasting Cucumber Soup! The Russian soldiers were looting and even now I can see them with watches on both arms up to their soldiers and their pockets filled with fountain pens and propelling pencils.

Soon after Liberation we returned to our old apartments and the other refuges who lived there, just moved on.

As you can imagine, this period was just huge confusion. My mother, my sister and I tried to find our few possessions and enquire after the survivors.

We had very little access to food and we certainly had no money, so my mother exchanged our few belongings for food.

School started again in April 1945 and we all exchanged many stories. Of course, our school was very badly damaged during the shelling and the air raids and alternative temporary accommodation was found.

In August 1945, when I was 9 years old, we learned of my father's death under terrible conditions, we were very poor and the future was uncertain.

In November 1948, at the age of 12, I had the opportunity to travel to France by myself and go to a Children's Home which was supported by American Jewish charity – once again by PEOPLE WHO CARED! I stayed in 2 different homes for 2 ½ years.

In March 1951, I arrived in Melbourne – another Children's Home for nearly 2 years. This Home was supported by the Australian Jewish Welfare – MORE PEOPLE WHO CARED! 3 more schools, learning a 3rd language and in 1953 I moved to live with my sister and started a new, more settled life.

At this stage, I would like to say a few words about Raoul Wallenburg. He was one of the most remarkable people of the 20th century. Being Swedish, coming from a neutral country, he was recruited by American Jewish and Swedish organisations to go to Budapest and organise a rescue mission for the remaining Hungarian Jewish population.

He was born to a very influential Swedish Christian family and diplomacy was second nature to him. He obtained a 'Diplomatic' position at the Swedish Embassy in Budapest and he used his influence, charm, cunning and cash to outwit the Nazis. He had been threatened with so-called 'accidents' but in those times of despair and against all odds, he succeeded more often than not. We learned of his deeds by word of mouth. He had given us hope and just the mention of his name was enough for us to realise that there were people around us who cared. He organised Diplomats from neutral countries to help him with his rescue mission. His cunning and personality helped to save close to 100,000 Hungarian Jews from certain death.

On the 17th January 1945 he disappeared and later we learned that he was arrested by the advancing Soviet troops on trumped up charges of espionage. They could not understand why a Christian Swede would want to come to Hungary just to save Jews. He must be a spy! The official Soviet version is that he died of a heart attack in a Moscow prison in 1947 – at the age of 35! However, no proof was ever offered. We now presume that he was executed at that time.

Today, he is remembered as a symbol of conscience of our free society, He is a Righteous Gentile – a term which is given by Jews to non-Jew, who saved Jewish lives. He is the recipient of many posthumous Honours including Honorary Citizenship of Israel, Canada and the United States of America. In the case of the U.S., only one other person has ever received this honour and that was Winston Churchill.

How did all this affect me? Firstly, I would like to say that every one of us, who has gone through this, would have been affected in a different way. And I respect every one of them. In my case, I lost my faith in God. On the day when I found out about my father's death, my reaction was that if God did exist, all of this would not have happened. However, I haven't lost my Jewishness. Also, I am extremely grateful to ALL people who helped – and there were a lot of them – from Raoul Wallenburg to Mrs. Molnar and her family who were hiding me.

Another aspect which affected me and still does affect me, sadly, it is a bitterness that I missed out on a normal childhood, I missed out on my parents and my parents have missed out on their children. What has the World learned from all this? Sadly, I have to say, very little. If we look around the World today, within the life of your generation, we see what happened in Cambodia, Rwanda and the former Yugoslavia – where they have invented new terminology for all this, and that is 'Ethnic Cleansing' – a most revolting term. Today, it is happening in parts of Asia and Africa like Sudan and Dafour, and tomorrow it will be somewhere else. I would like you to think of the extent of personal tragedies.

Fortunately, here in Australia we are not familiar with extremes of intolerance and racism, but we can make a significant contribution to decrease it in the rest of the World. This is far more important than cheap political point scoring

Not everybody can emulate Raoul Wallenburg, but we can all contribute to make this would a better place to live in.

Thank you very much[2].

---

2. A speech, circa 2009, regularly given by my long-time friend Peter Barta, in conjunction with the organisation Courage to Care. It's been told to hundreds of secondary students and importantly is still recounted today.

Read. Remember.

Taoism	Protestantism	Catholicism
Shit happens.	Let the shit happen to someone else.	If shit happens, you deserve it.
Judaism	Atheism	T.V. Evangelism
Why does shit always happen to us?	No shit	Send more shit.
Buddhism	Zen Buddhism	Hinduism
If shit happens, it is not really shit.	What is the sound of shit happening?	This shit happened before.

S

as in sex, love + marriage

'The best love affairs are those we never had.'
– Norman Lindsay

30% of the Australian adult population have never married. If a person is still single by the age of 30, the chance he or she will ever marry is now only 50%. Curiously it is not because men and women don't *want* to marry that they are staying single. It is that the social conditions which promoted marriage have changed radically over the past 25 years.

However, women still want to marry up – i.e., marry men older, taller, with better jobs, more income, better prospects than themselves. Men still want to marry down – to women who are smaller, younger, earn less than men do. The catch is that unmarried women are over represented in the high socio-economic groups and unmarried men over 30 swell the ranks of the physically and mentally ill, the unemployed, alcoholics and criminals and boost the statistics of industrial, road accident, suicide and other early death victims – not exactly the kind of men that those well-educated, intelligent career women want to marry.

Found in The Bulletin, 1989

Why is it so hard for women to find men who are sensitive, caring and good-looking? Because those men already have boyfriends.

~~~

'from George, with love together always'
on a small piece of paper between the double glazing of my window seat
Continental flight August 1990
New York to Seattle

~~~

There is nothing that can burst into flames and then be extinguished without a trace so easily as love.
found in book of Vietnamese stories,
September 1997

~~~

My wife is a sex object. Everytime I ask for sex, she objects
Les Damon

~~~

Using Viagra is like putting a flagpole on a condemned building
Harvey Korman

~~~

See, the problem is that God gives man a brain and a penis but only enough blood to run one at a time.

And yes, divorce: from the Latin word meaning to rip out a man's genitals through his wallet.
Robyn Williams

〰️

George Burns on sex:

My wife said she wanted to have sex in the back seat of the car, so she asked if I'd drive.

It isn't premarital sex if you have no intention of getting married.

Sex at 90 is like trying to shoot pool with a rope.

〰️

Woody Allen:

Sex without love is a meaningless experience, but as meaningless experiences go, it's pretty damned good.

〰️

*And a woman who held a babe
against her bosom said, Speak to us
of children
And he said:
Your children are not your children.
They are the sons and daughters of
Life's longing for itself.
They come through you but not from you.
And though they are with you yet
they belong not to you.
You may give them your love but not
your thoughts.
For they have their own thoughts.
You may house their bodies but not
their souls.
For their souls dwell in the house of tomorrow
Which you cannot visit, not even in
your dreams.
You may strive to be like them, but
seek not to make them like you.
For life goes not backward nor tarries
with yesterday.
You are the bows from which your
children as living arrows are
sent forth.*

      found in 'The Prophet'

The last time I was in a woman was the Statue of Liberty
Woody Allen

Marriage. The long and wounding road.

Marrying into money; it's the difference between working for the rest of your life, or working on your tan for the rest of your life.

If wives were a good thing, God would have one.
Sacha Guitry

To me the greatest latin lover was my dad, who married mother and was faithful to her until the day he died, 55 years later.
> Ricardo Montalban

Intercourse. Women need a reason; men need a place.

Bigamy is having one wife too many. Monogamy is the same.
> Oscar Wilde

If you marry for money you will earn every penny.
> P. McGraw

There are three kinds of woman. The beautiful, the intelligent and the majority.

Why do men have bigger brains than dogs? So we don't hump women's legs at cocktail parties.

Advice for the day: If you have a lot of tension and you get a headache, do what it says on the aspirin bottle, 'take two and keep away from children'.

The marriage is looking dicey when the husband phones home to say he'll be late for dinner and the answering machine says it's in the microwave.

When your wife runs off with another man, there is no better revenge than to let him keep her.

'My wife's an angel.'

'You're lucky, mines still alive.'

T

for travel.

'Are maps about people
or places?'
– Thea Astley

The following was handed to a flight attendant on a Qantas flight by an eight-year-old girl:

" dear Captain, my name is Nicola im 8 years old, this is my first flight and im not scared. I like to watch the clouds go by. My mum says the crew is nice. I think your plane is good. thanks for a nice flight dont fuck up the landing. "

'*The world is littered with travellers who asked one question too many, got a satisfactory answer and never went home again.*'

Jonathan Raban

Tourists don't know where they've been.
Travellers don't know where they're going.

    P. Theroux

    The Happy Isles of Oceania

I thought about becoming a travel agent, but then started having reservations ...

Met a traveller once, not so young, not so old, backpacking in Java. Said she wanted to keep travelling 'to meet everyone in the world'. (I'd like to think that she was still on the way to achieving that.)

Bali journal
1974

On crossing the Nullabor by bus – decided that having my camera stolen wasn't such a bad thing. How could you photograph this amazing vastness, this sameness, this timeless landscape of millennium and make it anything?

And waking early on the bus and saying 'Good morning, morning'.

Always like saying this when looking out at a new day.

And from same diary, June 1990
on crossing the Nullabor –

My sense of wonder seems to be enhanced every time I become aware of me loosing a little more ground with humanity in general – as technology increases, wonder seems to fade.

From diary June 1990, start of round the world trip:

It is with travel that we recognize our own foreignness; most clearly when in flight and away from home. The instability of meaning and the difficulty of translation between generations within as well as across different cultures and nationalities, all help us put the world into a better perspective.

Bali journal, 1999

With travel you have the opportunity to explore the micro-worlds found in each city – the cafes, the parks, the rivers. Plenty of opportunities to reflect on life, its sadness and the bolts of happiness that appear. To reflect on the tragedy of inevitable death that hangs over all of life.

Vietnam journal 1999

One of the delights of travel is that you know no-one and no-one knows you. That free and solitary passage among multitudes can never quite be attained at home; perhaps only in a foreign city where different language and different aspects of things turn the mind in upon itself for its needed reassurance and composure.

Paris Journal
June 2004

〰️
〰️

There is something divine in the sensation of your secret swim through this human ocean. You carry your own heavy and fragile burden of hopes, anxieties, joys, remorses and you know that you will not, from café crème at breakfast to café cognac at midnight, encounter anyone who has the faintest concern to share or jostle that curious load. So must the gods have walked among men ...

    Christopher Morley

    1926

Travel is fatal to prejudice, bigotry and narrow mindedness. Broad, wholesome, charitable views of man and things cannot be acquired by vegetating in one little corner of the earth all one's lifetime.

    from The Innocents Abroad

    Mark Twain

*W*ell, it's now nearly 4 months on the road & the diary extracts below have been compiled over the hours in planes & trains across the globe. It has just been one helluva roller-coaster ride from Asia to the Arctic Circle to California & across America to New York. A few days 'rest' here in Ridgewood with Susanne & John who have kindly leant me their pool & printer, both of which have made this letter possible!

9 May. Thanks to Lis, caught the old faithful Garuda Bird again to Bali. Decided that after some 15 years on this route that I should be eligible to join Garuda's 'Frequent Survivor' Programme. Started notes for my travel book, probably with that name!

12 May. After a few restful days, up at 4 a.m. with Jiwa to the Denpasar market for the restaurant order – hundreds of vendors & buyers in the half light, feverishly bargaining amongst the most amazing sounds & smells.

19 May. Having withdrawals from the Corvette – borrow Jiwa's convertible buggy, loaded surf gear & went to Medowi for 4 days. Shared waves and beers with Jun, a radical Japanese surfer with a Malibu.

1 June. Last day, always the time least looked forward to in Bali. It's been a good one – memorable dinners & trips with Annie & Perry, good surf & catching up with old friends. The leaving pains were eased with far too much G&T, beer, Cointreau & an excellent Balinese banquet at Kent's house to celebrate his birthday with Gillian & Jun. Jun decides after some beers that he is coming to surf Thailand with me tomorrow if he can arrange a ticket.

2 June. Yes, Jun is at departure lounge with a ticket! We arrive in Bangkok at 2 a.m. & somehow manage to find a boarding house that is open, check in & proceed to the 'No Name' Bar for some cold beer, reggae & pretty girls until 4.30 a.m.

Enough of Bangkok's heat & pollution by the next day & book the overnight bus to Phuket. Have my travellers cheques stolen whilst sleeping!!

12 June. Parted company with Jun in Phuket after a great week of surf, touring & partying & I flew to Bangkok for my connecting flight to London.

Phuket is probably one of the last bastions for REAL motorbike riding – spectacular jungle & mountain passes, a winding coastal road, Harley-style bikes, no helmets, sensible speeds, little traffic & willing Thai girls to go 2up – all for 500 Bht. a day ($30).

Staggered off the plane half asleep at 4 a.m. into the Abu Dhabi duty free & terminal. You felt about as welcome here as Salmen Rushdie in a Javanese furniture factory (sorry Perry), with lots of uniforms, weaponry & lecherous Arab salesmen eyeing white skins.

Back on the plane again; wondered if my luggage and surfboard were still with us?, remembered that nasi goreng was called 'Kow-phat' in Thailand, which could explain why it isn't as popular there; & before going back to sleep, finished 'A Time History of Briefs' by a Stephen Hawking, which left me confident in the engineering of Porsches & the dynamics of my surfboard, but in little else …

13 June. Thought I might get some cooler weather than the constant 30 of the last month, however London the same! Buy scalper ticket for Jackson Browne concert – front row seat at The Royal Albert Hall – great night, even greater venue!

14 June. Train to Cambridge for three hot days & really nice to see Aunt Jenny again & meet the natives there! Sad however that I should miss Harold by such a short time.

17 June. Take hovercraft and bus to Paris. Dinner at street café outside Notre Dame. Still 30 degrees.

Paris – the book says the city for all seasons. Maybe it is the city for all reasons? – serious people watching, elegant food & wine, elegant women!; a history of writers & thinkers; noble buildings. Remembered Sabine's comment in Bali – chiccy mickey. The most open rudeness, yet at the same time, he most wonderful joie-de-vivre.

18 June. Saturday night on the Left Bank for dinner, then to Crazy Horse for a fantastic show – it should be, they've been taking their clothes off now for 40 years!

19 June. Brunch on Bvde. St. Michelle, followed by five hour walk around the banks of The Seine to Eiffel Tower. Still 30c.

20 June. Pere Lachaise cemetery for lunch. More of an open-air museum & in the best company – Georges Bizet, Edith Piaf, Gertrude Stein, Oscar Wilde, Frederic Chopin & of course Jim Morisson. Chopin is still decomposing there …

21 June. I was running on empty in London after the J.B. concert, now I'm on sensory overload here in Paris – went to free Peter Gabriel open-air concert at Republique as part of the Paris Fete de La Music. Danced & drank with some pretty black girls.

22 June. It took 3 hours this morning to shower & pack, walk to my café for coffee & croissants, then walk to the Metro for the trip to Montpanasse station. It took the same time on the TVG to get from Paris to Bordeaux (500 kms) – great train & at around 200 k.p.h. you are in Bordeaux for lunch.

23 June. Only 1 ½ days in Bordeaux as the surf report is good. Take bus to Lacanau – two hours of good waves, but a little colder than Bali. Hired in-site tent close to beach with Sabine & Gabi from Germany – buy lots of fresh food and several 1.5 litre bottles of red wine & have a 5 star beach party!

26 June. Still surfing & drinking red, but time to get back for some culture in Bordeaux – a good wine & food festival is on.

28 June. Back to Paris for a couple more days; it is hard to resist. Go to haunting choir and concert recital in Notre Dame.

Benjamin Franklin pretty well summed it up – 'Every man has two countries: his own and France.'

1-5 July. Train to Komstad, Sweden. Good to see Tony, Sandra & Emelie again. Bring in hay for Sandra's grandparents, fishing on lake, visit the island of Oland, take Harley ride through some great rural scenery with Tony – & we manage to stay on!!

6-13 July. Take train from Komstad & travel some 1500 miles up to the Arctic Circle to the town of Kiruna. Meet Ake who kindly has place for me to stay. Great night life & bars here with impossibly attractive girls. Ake and I meet some, along with Anton Glazelius who was in the movie 'My Life As A Dog.' Home at 3.30 a.m. & the midnight sun is still up – it doesn't set until the 25th.

Overnight train back to Stockholm. Visit the Vasa Musuem & see Sweden's first submarine! Then back to Tony's for a few days before the long haul down to Frankfurt & across to the U.S.

14 July. Lost complete sense of time here, just a blur of trains, buses, hydrofoil, to Denmark, connecting trains, plane, pasta & champagne at 4 a.m. over somewhere & then a shuttle bus from L.A. Airport with Martin Gonner out of The Twilight Zone movie.

15 July. Yes, it's AMERICA THE MOVIE! Sit around the Hollywood hostel pool all morning with jet lag. The only hostel I've found with a pool – & only $15 a night.

Take afternoon walk to Hollywood Bvde & see Arnold Scwarznegger putting his paws into the wet concrete – the main doubt of the event expressed by the M.C., the Mayor of Hollywood, is whether Arnie will spell his name correctly? Fun afternoon with lots of glitz and stretch limos.

16 July. Train down to San Diego to Joan & John & great surf in California again – John is in a contest at Oceanside, still 30c & an endless summer!

18 July. Train to San Francisco & to great hostel. Take free tour with other hostellers to the bars & cafes in the Italian quarter, Northbridge for some wine & Californian pizza – the best!

20 July. The train from S.F. to Chicago breaks down in the Nevada desert & Amtrak put us up 5 star at the Nugget Casino in Reno – free use of restaurant, gym, pool & sauna.

21 July. A new train arrives for the most scenic route yet – through The Rockies. Pass the scenery & town where Thelma and Louise was filmed & go through the desert country where Butch Cassidy held up his first trains.

22-28 July. Arrive a day late in Iowa & meet up with Becky & Bob – lots of reminiscing about Aus. Just a great week with them, they were so kind – a full moon trip to Coralville Lake in their 1958 classic mahogany speed boat, a water skiing attempt, the best Mexican night with their friend Jackie, test drive her Miata, find some classic old Corvettes tucked away, bike riding, boating & a visit to the Amana & Amish towns – it all went too quickly.

29 July. Travelled on the train to Chicago with pretty South American, Monica and had fun over drinks planning our assault on New York city. Sadly this did not happen and her trip was cut short with news her father had had a car accident and she had to fly home. Shall follow her up when I get home.

30 July. Met at Newark by John Russo who stayed with me in Wye & he sure paid back the hospitality tonight. Dinner in New York at Richard Nixon's favourite hangout, then to the bars and cafes and a tour of Manhattan in all its glory.

31 July. Recovery Sunday around Susanne and John's pool with coffee, bagels & the New York Times.

1-7 August. I'm now a week behind plan, but who cares? New York has so much to offer – a world on its own. Went to the art deco Chrysler Building; there was a basement explosion there when we visited, the Empire State, the great Chelsea Hotel which housed the likes of Mark Twain, Tennessee Williams, Dylan Thomas, Jack Kerouac & Andy Warhol. Sid Vicious also murdered his girlfriend here for what it's worth. Bike riding through Central Park dodging joggers & roller bladers – the best park in the world with 800 acres in the heart of it all!

That's it so far – planning now for the trip back across California this week, then Hawaii & home. Not even sure where home is anymore!!

It's not over 'til it's over.

Cheers,

August diary & letter home
1994

... Travellers leave home to find out if they're really who they thought they were – or their mothers or spouses or friends insist they are – or actually somebody else.

... Moving around the globe for any other reason – to sleep in Hong Kong, to attend a business seminar in Singapore...may be fun, relaxing, instructive or even profitable, but it's merely displacement, not travel.

... Some have always travelled for salvation, of course, to Rome, Jerusalem and more generally in search of paradise. Indeed, in the 21st century that's really all that's left to us. Travellers travel to save their souls. Not believing very strongly in souls any more, we call it self-discovery.

... on the whole, it's best to leave home unaccompanied or with someone you can get rid of without too much trouble en route. It's also why we often travel best either when we're young and need to try different selves from the few on offer in Ballarat or East Bentleigh or else we're much older, feeling tired of who we've been for decades and vaguely nervous about the approaching deadline. It's also why sex and travel are so closely related and always have been...There is hardly a famous traveller you can mention who was not attracted by the possibility of sexual adventure while penetrating the unknown.

... Once you get home, after all, nobody will be remotely interested in what you did or what you saw. Why should they be? All they want to know is whether or not you 'had a good time', and your notion of 'a good time' is unlikely to be theirs. The best kind of traveller is a thief on the prowl for illuminating moments. You might like to keep a secret diary, but consider leaving the camera at home.

... but then ultimately travelling, unlike tourism, is just living more intensely, freed for a short time from the constraints of ... whoever it is we're accustomed to thinking we are.

Robert Dessaix
The Age 9/04

My Tips on Becoming an Airline Frequent Survivor, 2006

1. Forget travelling in particular seasons. It's always the Shoulder Season in Asia. For most of the year it is Armpit Season in Italy and France. If travelling to the UK, the winter months from August to May are cold and wet. During the summer months between the end of June and the beginning of July, it is almost as cold and wet.
2. Should you learn another language? Yes, so you can mumble something when approached by drug addicts and bums in the street. Also so as to make it quite clear that YOU ARE NOT AMERICAN should you be in a conflict zone. But always be courteous and have knowledge of customary greetings. Handshaking is generally used. In Bangkok and LA, 'hands up' is more widely practiced.
3. Allow $50 a day for Asia, $50/hour for Europe. Allow a little extra in the U.S. for tipping and mugging. And travel light, it means less to be stolen.
4. Hijacking. If you find a terrorist on board, exchanging names and addresses is not necessary. They are permitted to interrupt meal service and your in-flight movie. Try and fly the week after Ramadan as most hijackers have been fasting for the month and are more interested in food than foreigners.
5. Avoid trouble spots, always practice safe sex. Check for tanks and soldiers in the street before leaving your hotel each morning. Generally, elections in Thailand, Philippines and eastern countries are announced on the day. If you hear gunfire you will know an election is being held.

6. Most of Asia is populated with a diversity of religions – Muslim, Hindu, Tamil, Sikh – all living peacefully between riots.
7. Remember, Europe and the U.S. drive on the right. Japan and Australia on the left. Asia drives on both and in the centre.
8. Most places will have the world's largest, tallest or oldest something. McDonalds and Kodak will have strategic outlets there. Instead, go to less crowded places offering the 'second' of everything, eg the 2nd highest mountain, the 2nd oldest cathedral, the 2nd most tasteless hamburger.
9. How often does a jumbo jet crash? Just once.
10. And, if you look at all like your passport photo, then in all probability you need the journey.

So, why do we leave the comforts of our home and friends? It's not until you feel the sand on your feet in Hawaii, feel the tranquillity of Central Park in New York, the anxiety of 2 days and nights in a guest house in Harlem and then smelling the coffee as you exit the Metro in Paris.

It's just that you go. You go for the goings sake. As Jonathan Raban said '… travel is a kind of delinquency, more often rooted in the compulsion to escape the boredom and responsibilities of home than it is in any very serious desire to scale the Great Pyramid of Cheops or walk the length of the Great Wall of China.'

'… Going with a companion is cosy, but you might as well be with a coach party. The marital parliament has to sit in order to debate and settle the issue of lunch. You leave unexplored all the turnings you would have taken on impulse if you were alone. The stranger doesn't approach you in the dark bar, you don't get off at the wrong station, you don't go netting quail with the retired lieutenant of police… travelling in pairs and families is the continuation of staying at home by other means…Most damagingly is the luck and happiness department, you are simply not lonely enough… For spells of acute loneliness are an essential part of travel. Loneliness makes things happen.'

France Journal
Xavier's Apartment,
Suresnes, July 2006

On hotel life:
Have you noticed how odd people seek out even odder people as companions, possibly to show by contrast how normal they are?

Royal Grove Hotel
2016

So, travel well and remember:-

No expectations, no disappointments.

Bon séjour.

'You go away for a long time and return a different person – you never come all the way back.
    Paul Theroux
    Dark Star Safari

Hawaii Journal
July 2007

〰️

As Paul Theroux commented in his 'Ghost Train to The Eastern Star', travel is at its most rewarding when it ceases to be about your reaching a destination and becomes indistinguishable from living your life!

France journal
July 2008

〰️

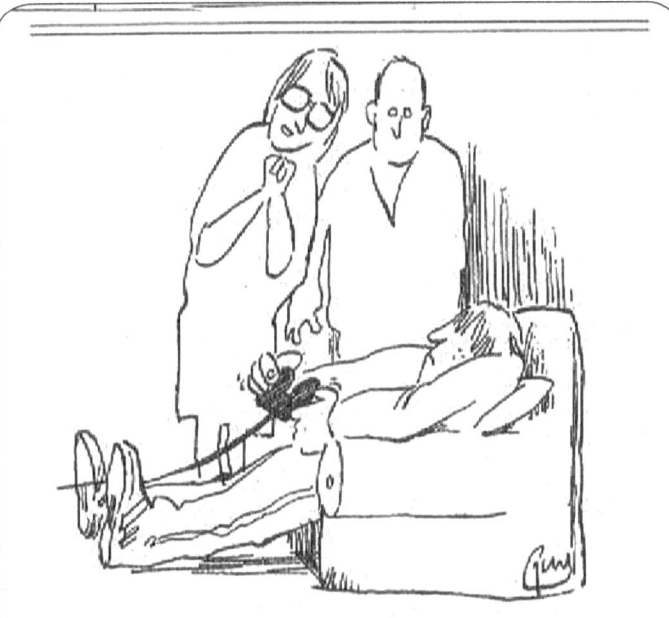

U

as in United States of America.

'Consider "the complex fate of being American"?'
– James.

USA

The US represents all that's right and all that's ill with the world, but you can't help getting caught up in its energy and enthusiasm. An extraordinary mix of first class service and gratuitous violence.

You soon learn about what's in the hearts and minds of most Americans – money! Yes, the best and worst of it all – bad beer, good wine. Best freeways, worst traffic. Worst coffee, best salads. Best rock music, worst country and western. Worst homeless, best homes. Worst take-away, best service. The fittest people, the fattest people. Classic old cars, ugly new ones.

Hawaii journal
July 1999

'*Anti-Americanism is the most dangerous global ideology. Today, all the totalitarianisms, the fundamentalisms, the anti-semitisms hide behind the banner of the fight against the USA.*'

French intellectual,

Bernard Henry-Levi,

US journal 2003

'The US has deployed forces overseas to deal with some sort of problem or another at least 2017 times since 1945. That's the world you're in. If you don't like it, fine. But that's the reality, and every problem we face, so do you. You can be an actor. Or you can stand aside and watch us, and either applaud or criticise. Or you can call for solutions everyone knows will never be implemented. Those, frankly, are the options.'

 Anthony GORDESMAN

 US strategic analyst

 New York journal 2003

Sometimes I think war is God's way of teaching Americans geography.
    Paul RODRIGUEZ

〰️

Most of the fun in visiting America comes from being close to its energy.

U.S journal
1997

〰️

This is America
This vast, confused beauty
This staring, restless speed of loveliness
Mighty, overwhelming, crude of all forms
Making grandeur out of profusion
Afraid of no incongruities
Sublime in its audacity
Bizarre breaker of moulds
    Amy Lowell, 1925

Have had this poem on file since 1990. Unexpectedly turned up in my paperwork and made me more comfortable being here – nothing really changes!

Sure, the Fords have got more forward, the rednecks appear redder, the food has got faster. The portions now even more fit the proportions of a super-sized population.

Yes, America the amiable monster. Where everyone is famous for 5 minutes. A lot of them seem to be at the end of their 5 minutes though – part of a people described as 'so restlessly creative as to be essentially destructive' by Louis Kronenberger.

Problem is, they just happen to be mostly nice as well, which makes it very hard not to like them, even with their '32 religions and still only one sauce'!

America, 'a great place to visit, but I wouldn't want it to live here' as Phillip Adams remarked.

Hawaii journal
June 2006

♒

*F*unny how life works sometimes. From the bleak Victoria coast one minute, to breakfast on the beach in Hawaii, brunch at Tavern On The Green in Central Park and not memorable dinner in Paris. The world's not such a bad place after all, but after a couple of weeks in the U.S you do begin to wonder.

Yes, the U.S. The best and worst of everything. Not sure about the trend with the waiters introducing themselves when they take your order – Weldon, Sheldon, Brandon. I seemed to get them all, but the best was 'Hi, I'm Chuck your somalier for the night'. Unfortunately he didn't see the dark side of this.

And some of the food is questionable. Upmarket gourmet hot dogs offered as 'Haute Dogs' and an inedible thing called a 'Croissan'wich' made you wish you'd already left for France.

Have a bit of a ritual now with New York, only 'cause it works. Arrive JFK early Sunday mornings. Minimal baggage-collection time, no queues, no traffic jams, plenty of taxis, you miss the first drive-by shooting. Collect the 2kg worth of New York Times, the travel section alone is the size of The Age and head for brunch in Central Park. Safe place now. The cocaine dealers are being encouraged to go organic and adopt the Fairtrade scheme. The muggers will accept VISA and Mastercard generally.

So much money now in the U.S from property, shares and bonds. Very few 2nd hand Camrys and Explorers in Manhattan these days. Sorry Simon and Perry, but Bentleys still rule!

Whereas New York used to be the Haves and the Have Nots, it now seems to be the Haves and Have Lots. Down on Wall Street it's the Haves and the Have Noughts. Up at Newport Rhode Island, the Haves and the Have Yachts…

Just a great few weeks though – excellent restaurants, great food, wine and service and you can just live with the 15% tip everywhere. Caught up with all the usual suspects, John and Susanne, Nick, Stephen and Lorraine, Donna. Thanks guys! Climbed Diamond Head volcano, ate at Hy's and Dukes, travelled to Cape Cod and Rhode Island and messed about amongst the boats. cycled around the Getty and Vanderbilt mansions, free champagne for vacating our table at Cipriani's, ate at The Bronx without getting shot.

But time to get out of Dodge last week and head for a 3rd world developing country; staying in Laetitia's apartment up on the hill in Montmartre overlooking Paris. Don't get confused with Paris Hilton or Paris Texas. It's a step back in time here after New York, but it doesn't take long to pick up the rules of the game there again – the protocol on the Métro, queuing at the bakery, or ordering a beer, not staring too long at all the pretty girls. Not looking too much like a tourist – you can tell other Americans and Australians, all with the multiple pockets on the shorts.

Paris Plage is operating again this summer, so I'm off with a book and lunch to secure my free deck chair on 'the beach'. Quite in Seine really …

US/France Dispatch
August 2007

♒

*H*ow did that old Beatles' song go? 'Happiness is a warm gun … bang bang …'

Well it certainly still is in the good old U.S of A. Last month, the worst mass shooting in the country's history, an ISIS supporter with an assault rifle kills and injures around 100 at a nightclub. Only seems like we were just getting over the horror of the 26 kids shot at the Sandy Hook school.

But these mass shootings are only a small part of the problem. In the 20 years up to 2012, some 325,000 gun killings in the U.S; now that's a lot of bullets. But only 540 of of these deaths were in mass shootings, with a large proportion of the rest being suicides the statistics show.

So the problem is not just your everyday, garden-variety military style assault weapon. It's the 300 million (300,000,000!!) other rifles and handguns in peoples homes and cars. That's 88 guns for every 100 Americans. Pretty impressive when you consider the next most gun-lovin' folk are from Yemen. They only boast 55 guns per 100.

But over the years of following this and with numerous trips, it's become painfully obvious that nothing's really changed or will change now or in the future.

The problem is too entrenched, the people love their firearms and have enormous support from both the courts and their beloved National Rifle Association. The good old NRA has about 5 million paid-up members with millions of others who take up the call when required, especially at times of legislature debate.

So, while the NRA with the blessing of the state courts, uphold the principle that the right to bear arms is essential to liberty, it then seems extremely difficult for gun-control advocates and groups to mount any serious legal challenges that guns may in fact undermine both liberty and democracy.

So, brace yourselves for further gun related events in the land of the free.

Paris
August 2016

V

as in Vietnam
and on the way to
Japan

Life is life
Fun is fun
But all is quiet
When the goldfish dies
   – Vinh Hung Hotel,
   Hoi An
   8/95

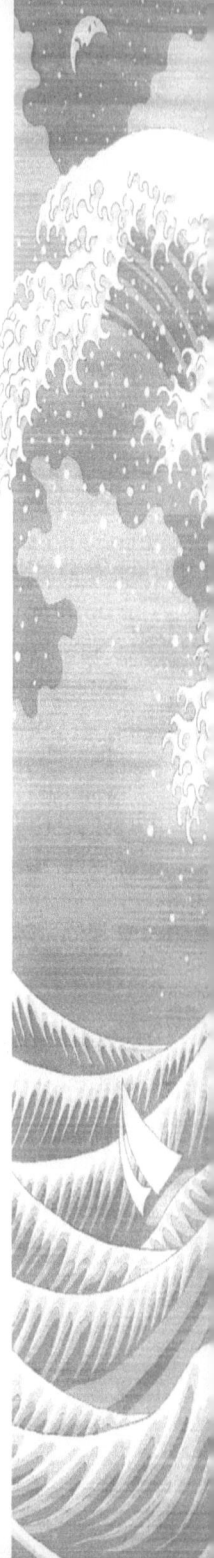

Vietnam was under French rule from 1883 to 1954, then divided into North and South, culminating in the fall of Saigon in 1975. Now with a population of 75 million, 3/5ths of them under 25 years old, with an average annual income of $US200.

Tourist appeal is here, everything inexpensive and antique with a single-track railway running up the coast and millions of bicycles. But this seems to be quickly giving way to scooters and trucks and, like Bali, you can see plastic about to take over from the leaves and paper wrapping of the food.

Mile after mile of family run stalls, it is a pervasively busy place, the Vietnamese generally finding life amusing rather than a serious business. So good to be here.

♒

So, it's during the crossing of a branch of the Mekong, on the ferry that plies between Vinh Long and Sadec in the great plain of mud and rice in southern Cochin-China. The Plain of the Birds.

... I look at the river. My mother tells me that never in my whole life shall I ever again see rivers as beautiful and big and wild as these, the Mekong and its tributaries going down to the sea, the great regions of water soon to disappear into the caves of ocean. In the surrounding flatness stretching as far as the eye can see, the rivers flow as fast as if the earth sloped downwards...

    Found in 'The Lover', Marguerite DURAS
Vietnam journal August 1995

♒

Meet the Vietnamese in number and its easy to conclude that the French and the Americans in Vietnam never stood a chance. A proud lot, they do nothing to puncture the notion that they are special and like to play-up the David-and-Goliath mystique for the benefit of foreigners and half-believe it themselves. How else would have they dared take on France, America and China?

If they turn out to be half as good at making money as they were at making war, Vietnam's people have a bright future.
    Found in The Economist
    August 1995

14.8.95. Lunch at Binh Pho,

9 Ly Chinh Thang St., Saigon. This quiet and ordinary soup shop, housed upstairs the secret headquarters of the Viet Cong in Siagon and was from here that their forward command was based during the Tet Offensive in 1968 and the attack was planned on the US embassy. Met the owner, Ngo Toai, now a legendary figure and highly decorated by the North Vietnamese Liberation Army, for his part in concealing the upstairs command office for so many years

Vietnam journal
August 1995

Classic cartoon from the 60s

18.8.95. Reunification Express. 20 hrs out of Saigon and on way to Danang. Hope our 20 Kph average will increase or I won't make Hanoi. Beautifully appointed train. Have a sleeper compartment with straw mats fitted to each of the six bunk beds. Asian-style toilet at one end of the carriage emptying to the tracks below. Wire grates instead of windows for the mortar shells and more recently children throwing stones. Walked the length of the train last night – only two westerners amongst the 300 odd locals on the trip – amazing stuff!

It's 6:30 am. Everyone has been up since 5:00 am. I've already had my language study for the morning from the two lovely girls from Danang Uni. Breakfast just served – Chinese tea in thimbles, soup for them, dark coffee and baguette with cheese for me. Viet Rail has catered well, apart from some fairly suspect meat and rice last night.

Petty crime is a problem on the train. You must tie your luggage to your leg while sleeping. People board the train at the various stops, then grab your bag and run. However I'm informed that with the speed of the express train, it is possible to chase the offender down the platform, retrieve your bag and then reboard the train.

Now 1 ½ hours out of Danang. Out of energy and paper and in need of a shower. Don't know how much further I will get, but at least want to see Hué and go metal-detecting around the DMZ. But it really doesn't matter because I'm coming back – the people, the food, the energy. Not to be missed. Marvellous stuff.

It's not over 'til it's over

journal entry, 'Reunification Express'
August 1995

It's been 12 months and now happy to be back in Vietnam. Some great travels up the coast but missed Hanoi by 600 Km as ran out of time and energy. So good to catch up with Ky Ky again at The Vinh Hung Hotel in Hoi An. Why this girl? Her beauty, her guitar playing, her martial arts, her French? Cook her ragu on request and tell her about my grilled snake dinner and being the first westerner to dine at the snake restaurant in My Tho last week. Refer menu for all the delicacies on offer.

Hoi An journal
August 1996

110	蛇粥	CHÁO RẮN SNAKE GRUEL	30.000	50.000
111	啄碎蛇肉	RẮN BẰM MINCED SNAKE	40.000	60.000
112	蛇羹	SÚP RẮN SNAKE SOUP	30.000	50.000
113	老薑煮蛇肉	RẮN NẤU GỪNG SNAKE COOKED WITH GINGER	40.000	60.000
114	蛇肉燉藥材	RẮN NẤU THUỐC BẮC SNAKE COOKED WITH MEDICINAL PLANTS	60.000	80.000
115	掠拌蛇肉	GỎI RẮN SNAKE MIXED WITH SALAD	40.000	60.000
116	烤蛇肉	RẮN NƯỚNG GRILLED SNAKE	40.000	60.000
117	香炒蛇肉	RẮN XÀO LĂN HALF DONE SNAKE	40.000	60.000

RÙA / TURTLE / 龜 類

118	龜肉撕絲	RÙA XÉ PHAY BOILED TURTLE TORN IN FONG PIECES	80.000	120.000
119	鹽焗龜	RÙA RANG MUỐI TURTLE ROASTED WITH SALT	80.000	120.000

NAI / SAMBAR DEER / 鹿 肉

120	瓦烤鹿	NƯỚNG VỈ GRILLED ON GRID	30.000	50.000
121	香炒鹿	XÀO LĂN HALF DONE	30.000	50.000

Đặt biệt: Kg.
RẮN HỔ MANG BIỂU DIỄN - CẮT TIẾT - LẤY MẬT UỐNG TẠI BÀN
Speciality:
COPPERHEAD - PERFORMANCE OF STICKING A COPPERHEAD FOR DRINKING ITS BLOOD CARD AND BILE ON THE SPOT (AT THE DINNER TABLE)
特別:
表演..割蛇取血, 取膽, 就席嚐試!

Left Vietnam two days ago for the 'Back To The Futon' stage of travel to Japan. Adjusting to $5 a minute here from $5 a day in Hoi An. Missing ky ky.³

Great Youth Hostel here in Kyoto, though twice as dear as usual hostels. But they don't come much better – a/c, hot spa with soap, shampoos, hair dryer, beer dispenser, bicycles and a tennis court.

Kyoto, impressive. Zen inspired gardens from the 1400's. Massive Shinto shrines, tea ceremonies and small inns. Myths and microchips. Where the Tokugawa shoguns are in combat with Colonel Sanders.

Hoi An/Kyoto journal
27.8.96

♒

31.8.96 Shinkansen Bullet Train. Can't remember how many years I've waited to ride this one. Only been on for one hour but already covered 200 Km of the 500 Km between Morioka and Tokyo. It should crank up to 300 Kmh once it gets going!

Scenery and villages along the rail a blur. But you can't help but wonder at the culture, the housing, the people, the strange customs – and that's just Australia. Appearing ignorant, not knowing the language, not being able to read road signs or restaurant menus and blowing your nose in public seems to please the locals and reassures them that they can spend many hours patiently explaining their customs to you while practicing their English

Japan journal 1996

---

3 Ky Ky, the little skylark. It's all become far too complicated over the last four years. 'if you leave home, I'm going to get sick and die' are the blackmail tactics from mother. Themes of arranged marriages, daughterly duty, visits to fortune tellers, superstitions and cultural differences – a lovely and great friend for the last few years and to remain that way for always. Like so many girls there, her life has been engineered for her according to suffocating social traditions. She chose life, learning and education, not teenage marriage, placing her on par, maybe above eligible male suitors. Happiness to you forever.

Hoi An
1999

4.9.96 Chiba. Been here at the surf beach now for a few days, Jun and his surfer mates have rented a beach front house. Typhoon has brought BIG surf. Waves a bit scary at first, but now smaller and glassy and great bunch of Jun's friends to surf with.

So, life's a beach again – waves, party, Japanese food, beer and plum wine. Pretty, pretty girls and sunshine. But I think I've earned this after negotiating Tokyo station. I'm sure most of the cities 12 million people were changing trains with me a few days ago – bit of a laugh really as you get pushed along with your surfboard by this wall of blue business suits.

My economic situation has improved here though – rent free beach house and nobody lets you pay for drinks which gets a little difficult when you want to repay some of their kindness and their forgiving of my endless breaking of their etiquette codes.

Taken to great bar last night in Onjuku. Everybody had a black belt in Karaoke except me and the nice girl who took me. great night despite the music and the five of us later taken to dinner by the bar owner at one in the morning.

Vietnam/Japan journal
1996

♒

8.9.96 Garuda 873, Tokyo to Bali. Reflections; Japan is certainly daunting. It's culture and customs certainly some of the most distinctive and complex anywhere. Biggest of the 4 islands is Honshu which consists of Tokyo and Mt. Fuji, Tokyo's suburbs seem to comprise the rest! Kyushu is the southernmost and translates to '9th' island, thus adding to further confusion. Lots of great food to try, doesn't have to be expensive in Izakaya and Economayaki restaurants and set lunch menus (ranchi Setto) – ramen, soba and udon noodles, yakitori, sashimi, nikijago, onigiri (rice balls filled with fish or veges). The Ako–Chochin (red lantern) bars also have yummy cheap eats.

Vietnam/Japan journal
1996

*I*t's taken me three visits over three years, but with the encouragement of three Canadian doctors staying at my hotel, its time to dine at one of the 'Union of Dog Meat Factories' restaurants in Hanoi.

We all approach the menu with some apprehension. Seven dishes offered. We are the only westerners seated and a neighbouring table of Vietnamese offers some loose translations – dog's feet broth, dog meat stew, meat balls, grilled dogs meat or steamed. We quickly order four beers. Don't think I can go for the tasty pair of dog feet in a hot bowl of broth. My meat balls, grilled, arrive with an accompanying sauce. Overpowering smell of citronella and dreadful taste to match. But the meat on it's own, quite acceptable and spicy. But never again.

Hanoi Journal
August 1997

Postscript

Vietnam journal, July 2016

Fly from Ho Chi Minh City to Hoi An. Lovely reunion with Ky Ky after many, many years. She's had success, happily married with two daughters and runs rental villas and a tailoring business in town. So happy to see her well and successful. We go to great dinner at her girlfriend Vy's 'Cargo'. (Vy has three restaurants in Hoi An – She's one of Vietnams's top chefs and has now opened House of Hoi An restaurant in Melbourne)

Việt Nam News — 1997

Gastronomic quarters thrive

by Binh Nguyên

HCM CITY — Newspapers and magazines are full of stories about the amazing food that is available in HCM City. However, as the city is full of new gastronomic quarters, more and more kinds of food keep being added to the list.

As a result of this country's fast-paced economic development, Sài Gòn's restaurant scene is changing quickly. People who leave the city for even a short time may feel lost upon their return.

For a start, let's examine some of the more unusual types of food. In Hà Nội, the "Union of Dog Meat Factories" is well-known. A long time ago, HCM City also had the same kind of "union." Dog meat restaurants are not only known to north Vietnamese people living in HCM City but also to people from the center and even to natives of Sài Gòn.

The best known dog meat quarter is in the Ông Tạ region of the Tân Bình District. Billboards for these shops do not advertise seven or nine dishes but proudly boast of "eleven dishes." The owner of the Hai Mơ shop explained that his restaurant used to sell only seven dishes but now serves nine or 11 dishes.

The new dishes are prepared according to his customers' suggestions. One such example is the tasty dish named "dog's feet broth," which his customers refer to as "a pair of brakes." Who can resist a pair of dog's feet in a hot bowl of broth?

Since the price of streetfront houses continues to rise, many dog meat businesses have decided to cooperate. Groups of vendors rent several small houses in an alley off Nguyễn Thị Minh Khai Street, near the Thị Nghè bridge and in a large plot of land near railway gate no.6 in Phú Nhuận.

It's strange that in this time of fierce competition, many businessmen choose to sell the same kind of food in the same street. Nonetheless, the dog meat shops

With tables and chairs on the pavement, these informal restaurants are midnight.

are grouped together beneath advertisements that proclaim their dishes as being "good for men's health".

Each afternoon, after working hours, these quarters are crowded with customers. The clientele range from cyclo drivers to public employees and rich businessmen equipped with mobile phones. They all come to these shops in order to enjoy delicious food prepared from dog meat "chả chìa, rựa mận, xáo măng..."

Each of these quarters has its own speciality. If you want to eat the best rựa mận (dog meat stew), you should come to the Ông Tạ quarter.

The sauce that accompanies the dog meat is the best to be found in HCM City. You will not forget the sauce's special citronella flavour. For steamed dog meat, nowhere can surpass the Thị Nghè bridge quarter. Before eating the tender meat with its delectable, crispy skin, the morsel should be dipped in some mouth-watering black prawn paste.

Sài Gòn boasts a wide range of food which people love to eat just for fun. These include many kinds of popular foods prepared from rice noodles, such as bún thang, chicken rice noodles or eel rice noodles. Adventurous diners can try such strange foods as mountain-lizards fried in butter, which are sold at a low-budget shop named Th.Th. on Sương Nguyệt Anh Street. Turtle eggs stewed with Chinese medicinal herbs are popular at the Bình Quới Restaurant in the Bình Thạnh District.

Those who have less exotic tastes could visit Ngô Thời Nhiệm Street. This area is known for its "beef steam boat." "Goat meat steam boat" can be found in the Bàu Sen quarter on Lê Hồng Phong Street, as well as on Nguyễn Công Trứ Street. This last location offers delicious toasted goat meat.

Connoisseurs in Sài Gòn are probably used to visiting seafood restaurants on Thi Sách Street, District 1. These shops offer fresh crabs, shrimps, oysters and more. Prices are much cheaper than those at fancy restaurants.

W

as in wine, food and cheese

or a case of food-in-mouth disease

Champagne for my real friends; real pain for my sham friends.
Francis Bacon,
English painter

Wine is one of the most civilised things in the world and one of the natural things that has been bought to the greatest perfection. It offers a greater range for enjoyment and appreciation than possibly any other purely sensory thing that can be purchased.
　　Ernest Hemingway

' *There is something about lunch in France that never fails to overcome any small reserves of willpower that I possess. I can sit down, resolved to be moderate, determined to eat and drink lightly, and be there three hours later, nursing my wine and still open to temptation. I don't think it's greed. I think it's the atmosphere generated by a roomful of people who are totally intent on eating and drinking. And while they do it, they talk about it; not about politics or sport or business, but about what is on the plate and in the glass. Sauces are compared, recipes argued over, past meals remembered, and future meals planned. The world and its problems can be dealt with later on, but for the moment, la bouffe takes priority and contentment hangs in the air. I find it irresistible...*

    Peter Mayle

    Toujours Provence

'*Soup should be served at a formal meal, and must at least be tasted, it is rude to leave it untouched. By this means we delicately ensure that everyone present is fortified before wine is served; we also enforce the highly civilised impression that nobody present is anxious to get started on the wine.*'

From The Rituals of Dinner by Margaret Visser
Hanoi journal 2003

In vino veritas
Truth in wine

≈

The 'www dot com' of wine (wonderful world of wine). Some interesting vignettes, collected over a 40 year association with the grape.

The French generally drink their wines far younger than we do – they say it's an English affectation.

Churchill must go down as one of the greatest heroes of the drink. His habits were admirable. A Foreign Office official described a dinner with Churchill as a 'varied and noble procession of wines of which I could not keep pace – Pol Roger, claret, port, brandy, Cointreau . 'I have taken more out of alcohol than alcohol has taken out of me' was one of Churchill's great bon mots.

The differences between the great Bordeaux districts in the Haut-Médoc. These are the Margaux, the St.-Julien and the Pauillac – the Margaux has a gentle femininity, the St.-Julien an austere femininity, while the Pauillac has all the virtues.

And of Château Y'quem? It is to dessert wines what Krug is to Champagne. One hundred and fifty pickers harvest the grapes one by one. It is said to be the only place where all the wine-making machinery is made of wood, so that no metal comes into contact with the wine in case it should affect the taste. The most satisfactory way of drinking it is with a simple peach.

One of the greatest advertising cons in history has to be the link between champagne and celebration. It has been rooted in the public consciousness for so long that it has become an unchallenged cultural ritual. But for many drinkers it is an irritation. If you are one of the red brigade, you cringe when you hear the cry of 'this calls for a celebration'. Invariably, out comes a bottle of luke warm fizz, half of which spills down the side of the bottle or the glass, leaving everyone standing around with a half filled flute of carbonated Blue Nun.

The fact is, people who take a real interest in wine, prefer red. The reasons are obvious. There are so many more blends. It lends a conviviality to a meal which a crisp white cannot begin to match. It looks deeper, warmer, more interesting, more giving. It comes in larger glasses. But the greatest argument for red against white is that it boasts the stamp of medical approval – a glass or two a day loosens the arteries and is good for the heart. So, just remember at the next celebration when the champagne is called for, to pronounce 'Better red than dead!'

Paris journal 2005

My definitive list of Paris Winebars, as at 2006

WILLI'S	13 rue des Petits-Champs
JUVENILES	47 rue de Richelieu
LE RUBIS	10 rue du Marché-St Honoré
AUX BON CRUS	7 rue des Petits Champs
LE VERRE VOLÉ	38 rue Oberkampf
CAVE LA BOURGOGNE	144 rue Mouffetard
LES VINS DES RUES	21 rue Boulard
LE SANCERRE	22 ave Rapp
AU SAUVIGNON	80 rue des St. Péres

(TO BE ADDED TO EACH YEAR)

France journal 2006

*J*acqueline Friedrich writes in the Herald Tribune in November 2005, that we are living in a golden age of French wine quality, despite a well publicised crisis in sales.

So, time to help sales and visit the worlds best wine shop in Paris, Lavinia. Over 6000 wines on offer over two levels with a great bar and bistro on level three. Wine here by the glass, or you can purchase a bottle downstairs and consume it with lunch there. No corkage either.

Southern Rhone wines have now been brought into the modern era. Producers such as Marcel Richaud doing plush Cotes du Rhone and Cairanne reds with great fresheners and succulent ripe fruit, a welcome change from the scratchy, leathery standard Rhone wines of the past. Here's some other good ones to try:

Domaine de la Louvetrie, a dry muscadet.
Domaines Gramenon, Dard and Ribo.
Domaines Viret, Yves Cuilleron.

I like to think it is a triumph of human cunning that we eat oysters when they have surely developed an evolutionary survival strategy to make themselves look disgusting ...//

... But the oyster sensation – it is more than a taste – is so potent that it also throbs with meaning. It signifies breaching the faddishness of childhood, becoming adult or, to put it another way, discovering sex. Ugly but sexy, oysters are the Jean-Paul Sartre of the edible world, which brings me to the point at the end of a long chain of association, namely that I like eating them in Paris more than anywhere else ...//

... The French oyster season runs from roughly October to March, and for most of this period great, tottering piles of oyster encrust the city ...//

... Paris oysters typically come from the three great French production areas of Arachon, Cancale and Marennes-Oleron... Oysters are graded in France according to a system similar in its complexity to the country's wine appellations. The difference is that there is no oyster equivalent to plonk: all are good, when very fresh, but the first thing to know is that France cultivates two species of oyster. The ubiquitous Pacific variety, also known as the huitre creuse or simply creuse (referring to its concave inner shell), accounts for 90 per cent of production. The creuse is simpler tasting than the other variety, the huitre plate (meaning 'flat') which was the original French oyster. Reduced by disease and overharvesting, and being relatively difficult to cultivate, it is now rare ...//

... A further category, concerns the oysters' period of maturation in estuarine waters – 'claires' – where they are placed before being finally taken to market. The difference concerns the density of the oysters on the riverbed and the amount of time they spend there. 'Pousses en claires' are the most privileged, with plenty of nutrient-rich water to each oyster and around four months to enjoy it, followed by 'speciales de claires' and 'fines de claires', this last being the everyman oyster most people eat ...//

... Au naturel is the way almost all oysters are eaten in France, although you may get a sauce mignonette – a dressing of red wine vinegar and chopped shallots – if you order them in a bar. Rye bread spread with unsalted butter helps to clear the palate between each deliciously salty submersion ...

    found in Paris is Heaven for Oyster-Lovers
    by Simon Busch, 17/3/07
France Journal 2008

A quick overview of the evolution of Australian wine:

1950s- Probably the start of me being weaned off those lime spiders with the introduction of Barossa Pearl.

1960s- What's not to remember about Ben Ean Moselle and the Kaiser Stuhl 'Cold Duck'. But Coonawarra did appear on the wine map. Wynns, Lindemans, Penfolds and Mildara all cultivating that beautiful red dirt.

1970s- A few more shockers appeared in the hotel bottleshop -Blue Nun, Liebfraumilch, Black Tower. And wine consumption doubled with the 'wine in the box'. The cask set a new standard and brings back 'a bladder full of memories.'

1980s- Plenty of good and bad reds and whites. The over-oaked chardonnays confirmed my membership of the ABC club.

1990s- Australia starting to get serious. The word 'terroir' snuck in, along with new grape varieties of sangiovese, nebbiolo, barbera etc.

2000+- the stock and trade Shiraz and Cabernets just getting better and better, alongside lots of exciting new exotics. Robotic tractors being developed that harvest and prune, while the French are experimenting with tractors that can measure baumé, ph and acidity!

Where would we be without wine, glorious wine?

Ergo Bibamus!

France Diary, 2015

Les Marchés

Paris is dotted all over with lively street markets. I've made a point over the last twenty years to try and visit most, whether it be to try that bag of cherries that might be the last of the season, or to get that ready-roasted quail and box of baby potatoes for lunch that day.

This list is by no means exhaustive and it's just a matter of selecting the market that happens to be where you are at the time.

They are all excellent and truly what makes Paris one big village.

- Marché Montorgueil.
  In the 2nd arrondissement, colourful and noisy fruit and vegetable sellers, good artisan bread since 13th century! The street is lined with good cafes and don't go past one of the oldest and best patisseries in Paris, Stohrer (health warning alert!)
- Marché Mouffetard (5e)
- Marché Monge (5e)
- Marché St. Quentin (10e)
  Beautiful iron and glass covered enclosure built in 1880s.
- Marché Bastille
- Marché rue de Bretagne

Paris Journal
2013

Observations from a café table, Paris

Cafes still overflow for every lunch and dinner. For some reason the French still see middays as the main meal. Possibly this helped by the fact that they get a subsidised meal voucher for lunch from their employer?

A visit to a supermarket or street market still highlights after all our advancements at home, how far behind we are with cheese for example and the presentation levels of other produce.

And the French reds and whites? The good ones show an elegance and lower alcohol level that generally our Australian wines don't possess. Our reds here are known to be well concentrated, but high in alcohol, too heavy, rich and dense with little of the elegance displayed in the good French reds.

Paris journal
2016

I like the observations from the French author Jean-Francois Revel that there is a 'grande cuisine internationale'; it so happens to be French.

This is not because it has invaded the world but rather because it has rethought-rewritten the food of all regions and countries. For the French are foodists rather than foodies. With Zola and Rabelais, alimentation was for the 'ventre', not the 'tête',

Bali journal
2017

X

as in Xenophobia

and other words
I never knew the
meaning of.

So, depending on what you are suffering from, here's a helpful guide to some new medications that turned up in where else?, the U.S. back in 2003

U.S. Diary
2003

- Confusadril
- Preventidrool
- Revoltin
- B-Itch
- Preventafit
- Amexx
- Hypochondriax
- Que Sera Serum
- Conundraderm
- Accidentiprone
- Mindbenderine
- Prozenconz

The word for torch is the most beautiful in French – 'chalumeau', a close rival to Edgar Alan Poe's proposal for the most beautiful sound in English, 'cellar door'.

    found in Paris, 2003

The Washington Post runs two contests a year. The first, where readers are asked to supply alternate meanings for various words, and a second contest where one letter is changed and a new definition supplied.

A few of the winning words in 2002 with alternate meanings:

- Coffee (n.) a person who is coughed upon.
- Abdicate (v.) to give up all hope of ever having a flat stomach.
- Lymph (v.) to walk with a lisp
- Rectitude (n.) the formal, dignified demeanour assumed by a proctologist immediately before he examines you.
- Circumvent (n.) the opening in the front end of boxer shorts.
- Frisbeetarianism (n.) the belief that, when you die, your soul goes up on the roof and gets stuck there.
- Pokemon (n.) a Jamaican proctologist.

And some nice entries from the second contest:

- Intaxication: euphoria at getting a tax refund, which lasts until you realize it was your money to start with.
- Giraffiti: Vandalism spray painted very high.
- Sarchasm: The gulf between the author of sarcastic wit and the person who doesn't get it.
- Inoculatte: To take coffee intravenously when you are running late.
- Hipatitis: Terminal coolness.
- Osteopornosis: A degenerate disease.
- Ignoranus: A person who's both stupid and an arsehole.

(The last was revealed as the pick of the literature!)

English as she is spoke

I take it you already know
of tough and bough and cough and dough.
Others may stumble but not you
on hiccough, thorough, laugh and through.
Well done! And now you wish perhaps
To know, of less familiar traps.
Beware of heard. a dreadful word
that looks like beard, and sounds like bird
And dead, it's said like bed not bead,
For goodness sake's, don't call it deed!
Watch out for meat and great and threat
(They rhyme with suite and straight and debt)
A moth is not a moth in mother
Nor both in bother, broth in brother,
And here is not a match for there
Nor dear and fear for bear and pear
And then there's rose and close and lose
Just look them up – and goose and choose
And cork and work and card and ward
And font and front and word and sword
And do and go and thwart and cart.
Come, come, I've hardly made a start
A dreadful language? Man alive!
I'd mastered it when I was five.

ALTERNATIVE MEDICAL DICTIONARY

Artery	The study of paintings
Bacteria	Back door of a cafeteria
Barium	What doctors do when patients die
Bowel	A letter like a, e, i, o, u
Caesarian Section	A neighbourhood in Rome
Cat Scan	Searching for kitty
Cauterise	Made eye contact with her
Coma	A punctuation mark
D&C	Where Washington is
Dilate	To live longer
Enema	Not a friend
Fester	Quicker
Fibula	A small lie
Genital	Not a Jew
Hangnail	Coat hook
Impotent	Distinguished, well known
Labour Pain	Getting hurt at work
Medical Staff	Doctor's cane
Morbid	A higher offer
Nitrates	Cheaper than day rates
Node	Was aware of
Outpatient	A person who has fainted
Pap Smear	A fatherhood test
Pelvis	A cousin of Elvis
Recovery Room	Place to do upholstery
Rectum	Dang near killed 'em
Secretion	Hiding something
Seizure	Roman emperor
Tablet	A small table
Terminal Illness	Getting sick at the airport
Tumour	More than one
Urine	Opposite of 'You're out'
Varicose	Nearby
Vein	Conceited

I took it upon myself in the seventies to read the dictionary. Here are a few words that presented themselves with interest:

AENEON – an age of the universe, immeasurable period.

AFFLATUS – communication of supernatural knowledge.

AHIMSA – non-violence or non killing – the highest form of duty.

APPERCEPTION – mind's perception of itself.

BENTHAMISM – greatest happiness of the greatest number.

BENTHOS – flora + fauna found at the ocean bottom.

BERKELEIAN – denying the objective existence of the material world.

BONISM – doctrine that the world is good, but not the best possible.

CACHEXY – ill-conditioned state of body or mind.

CACOGRAPHY – bad handwriting or spelling.

CATALEPSY – suspension of sensation + unconsciousness accompanied by rigidity of the body.

CHOTAHAZRI – light early breakfast.

CLARET – 'tap one's claret' – make his nose bleed with blow of fist.

COMESTIBLE – thing to eat.

CORRUGATOR – muscle that contracts the brow in frowning.

CRYPTAESTHESIA – supernormal knowledge, whether telepathic or clairvoyant.

DEAMBULATION – walking.

DEGLUTITION – swallowing.

DEJECTA – person's or animal's excrements.

DISCALCEATED – barefooted.

DOLCE FAR MENTE – pleasant idleness.

ELYSIUM – place, state of ideal happiness.

EMUNCTORY – of nose blowing.

FROEBELISM – education of young children on the kindergarten system.

GEOPHAGY – dirt eating.

GUDDLE – catch fish with the hands.

HODIERNAL – of the present day.

HOGMANANY – last day of the year.

HORRIPILATION – goose-flesh; bristling of the skin.

HOURI – voluptuous, beautiful woman.

LAUDATOR TEMPORIS ACTI – one who prefers the good old days.

LIMITARIAN – holder of doctrine that only a limited number of mankind is to be saved.

MELIORISM – doctrine that the world may be made better by human effort.

NATIVISM – doctrine of innate ideas.

NEPHOLOGY – study of the clouds.

NESTOR – wise old man.

NONAGENARIAN – person between 89 + 100 years old.

OBJECTIVISIM – doctrine that knowledge of non-ego is prior + superior to that of the ego.

OCEANID – ocean nymph of Greek mythology.

OPSIMATH – one who learns late in life.

PABULUM – food.

PAGETT, M.P. – traveller who expects to know all there is to know of a country in a few months.

PHRONTISTERY – place for thinking in, thinkery.

SCATOPHAGOUS – feeding on dung.

SCIAMACHY – fighting with shadows.

STERNUTATION – sneezing, sneeze.

Y

as in

You are where you eat.

And the Hawaiian guy who said they don't eat until they are full – they eat until they go to sleep.

Hawaii journal
2003

When hungry, consider ordering a piece of fish and a maximum of chips?

"She thinks I think it's real latte, but I know decaf when I taste it."

*T*he dining experience at the Hanoi dog restaurant this month has helped formulate another money-making venture to discuss with Ivan Cave, my financial mentor, on my return.

Having observed the popularity of the dog restaurants in both Saigon and Hanoi, surely the time is right in Australia for a chain of similar restaurants to take on the big boys, eg Mut Donalds or Kennel Sanders?

With the recent spate of dog attacks in Melbourne and the outbreak of Mad Cow disease in Britain, these restaurants could again make people more comfortable with meat eating, knowing that if a dog bites them they will have some redress at a restaurant.

So why is it the right time? The world is overpopulated with dogs. They are everywhere, they're like sheep. God, I've just spent a month hop-scotching around their turds on the footpaths of Paris. There are also far too many dog shows and fox hunts, not to mention the so called 'trained' dogs that walk and piss over your luggage at every airport. Even Hugh Worth and Lord Smith tell us they have more dogs than potential owners. They alone could provide enough meat to satisfy all the purveyors of pooch and lovers of canine cuisine out there.

So, what's the plan? Basically, with Ivan's money, the 'Dogs On The Run' outlet would be opened and franchised, or possibly leashed? Children will be hounding their parents for this new taste sensation and the popularity will fund the next outlet. Advertising and catchy jingles such as 'How much is that doggy in the window?' will follow. Sung by Ronnie Barker?

Suggested menu:

1. Snacks
    » Sausage Dog Rolls
    » German Shepherd Pies
    » Spot Specials

2. Meals
    » Big Muts
    » Pooched Eggs
    » Pizza Weimaraner
    » Coq 'A Spaniel

3. Desserts
    » Dog in a Pond
    » Fresh Paw Paw

4. Drinks
    » Fruit Lassies
    » Kennel Coughee
    » Robur tea (for people with a lisp)

5. Restrooms for Male, Female and Disabled– designated as Shitzus?

Vietnam Journal 1997

Some classic New York eateries from New York journal July 1999

✓   Cucina di Pesci, 87 E 4th Street.
In the East Village and away from touristy Little Italy. Peasant-style pastas, been there forever and great value.

✓   Ferrara Espresso Bar, 195 Grand St.
Been there since 1892, first espresso machine in USA and still pulling excellent coffee.

✓   Old Town Bar, 45 E 18th Street.
Built in 1890's, typical wild west pub with wooden booths etc.

✓   Lexington Candy Shop, 1226 Lexington St at 83rd St.
Been there since the 1920s, New York last authentic malted milkshakes in classic diner environment.

〜〜
〜〜

Some classic Paris bistros, not to be missed.

From France journal, August 1999

- Au Gourmet de I'lsle, 42 rue St. Louis-en-I'lsle
- Au Pont Marie, 7 Quai de Bourbon
- Lescure, 7 rue de Mondovi
- Le Petit Saint-Benoit, 4 rue St. Benoit
- La Fontaine de Mars, 129 rue Saint-Dominique
- Le Bateau Lavoir, 8 rue Garreau
- Au Pied de Fouet, 43 rue de Babylone

Would you say that I'm arrogant? I hope so and if not, I'm certainly going to try and perfect it.

The Parisians are bastards. I was told this at lunch yesterday by one at the 100-year-old Bouillon Chartier. They're arrogant and they get away with it, 'cause they can. In a city with the most eclectic mix of architecture, fashion, food and culture, all served up with that wonderful dash of arrogance that only Parisians can carry off.
On leaving Paris on TGV to Rennes to visit Gaelle
12 August 2002

It doesn't get any better. Anywhere. At least not in this lifetime. If, for any reason, this should be my last writing, know that I've gone to meet the family, the happiest and most contented and well fed that I could have wished for.

For it has been said that Paris is a harlot of a city. So open your heart to her, lay bare the contents of your wallet, and be seduced.

Although strongly Catholic, religion, like everywhere, is dwindling. Food and wine are the religions of France.

They would rather sit and eat than kneel and pray.

The sermons are short, the tables long.
France diary, 2002

Bon Appetite, Mon Appetite!

Think it was De Gaulle who said 'how can you possibly govern a country that produces 360 different cheese?' Not to mention the thousands of wines from 875,000 wine growers!

And the restaurants, cafes and bistros – you thought New York was crowded with 17,000 restaurants? Serious business here in France – serious eating, not to be messed with. Move over McDonalds! One restaurant I know of has no less than 200 champagnes on its wine list – my god!

The atmosphere of eating and drinking here in France is unequalled – the definitive 'long lunch', the home of slow food.

The Michelin Guide is the definitive reference for where to eat. One star indicates good food and in a pleasant environment and worth a stop if you are in the area. Two star means it is worth a detour. Three star means leave the children at home, sell the car and cross the continent to get there; the food will be out of this world. So will be the prices!

So, what the hell is it all about – haute cuisine? Bistro cuisine? Nouvelle cuisine? Even the French friends I asked seemed bewildered.

Seems like 'grande cuisine' is the same as 'haute cuisine'. Flavoured and favoured now by the few. A big dinner for those who enjoy being lifted up from the dining table at the end of the meal.

So, Nouvelle Cuisine is the go. Emerged in the '70s, along with aerobics, heart disease and cholesterol. Cut down the portions and keep the butter, cream and fat to a minimum.

But I think my heart lies with bistro cuisine. Dark coloured walls, smoke-stained ceilings, a zinc covered bar being supported by a mixed group of garrulous regulars clutching glasses of Beaujolais and Cotes du Rhone as plates of rabbit and lamb ragout, cheese and breadstick are shipped between them by stern faced waitresses from another era. When the cigarette smoke gets a little too thick, take your coffee and sit at an outside table.

The bistros are in plague proportion in Paris and found everywhere else in France. In Lyon they are called 'bouchons' and in Strasbourg 'winstubs' (wine bars). Although these small family run affairs have been threatened by fast food outlets and snack bars, they are far from extinction and the generally excellent family fare can be consumed easily on a daily basis with no fear of monotony or exceeding your credit card limit.

Yes, as Hemingway said 'Paris is a movable feast'.

Lyon Journal
August 2000

Z

as in

Zen and the Art of
no garbage can

*H*ome is where your friends are.

IF A MAN DOES NOT KEEP PACE
WITH HIS COMPANIONS
PERHAPS IT IS BECAUSE
HE HEARS A DIFFERENT DRUMMER.
LET HIM STEP TO THE MUSIC
WHICH HE HEARS,
HOWEVER MEASURED OR FAR AWAY.

Since everything's so meaningless, we might as well be extraordinary
  Nietzsche

There are only two times in life; there's now and there's too late.

The dance is now.

The purpose of life is in the search.
  Gabriel Marquez

On Margot Fonteyn; she says that travel is essential, that spending money is essential too, and that the only thing to do when one has money is to spend it. You have to discover what 'comforts' are to your taste and then arrange to have them. Travel.

Fonteyn says 'You mustn't shut yourself up in a closed world, not even intellectually. My ideal is to be at home everywhere, in every place, in every environment. Our education, station and snobbery tend to imprison us in a world of our own and cut us off from life.'

    found in amongst articles by Marguerite Duras
Bali journal 1996

Marguerite Duras interview with French actress, Melina Marcouri:
To be at home what does that mean to you?

'At home, is people not a place. When I'm with people with whom I can relax and say whatever is on my mind, I'm at home.

What I'm proudest of is that I own nothing. That's a terrible thing to be proud of, isn't it? The idea that one can do without ownership in a world where everyone wants nothing else.'

Bali Journal 1996

≈

When they discover the centre of the universe, a lot of people will be disappointed to discover they are not it.
Bernard Bailey

Old Japanese saying:

A man away from home has no neighbours.
Hoi An journal
1997

'The Cato institute has an unusual political cause – which is no political cause whatsoever ...

We have no ideology, no agenda, no catechism, no dialectic, no plan for humanity. We have no 'vision thing' as our ex-president would say, ...

All we have is the belief that people should do what people want to do, unless it causes harm to other people. And that had better be clear and provable harm. No nonsense about second-hand smoke or hurtful, insensitive language, please...

I don't know what's good for you. You don't know what's good for me. We don't know what's good for mankind. And it sometimes seems as though we're the only people who don't ...'

P.J. O'Rourke on the Cato Institute, 1993

France Journal, 2000

You might not know always where you are going but you always end up where you're meant to be –

'*They share with each other, (citizens of nowhere) across all the nations, common values of humour and understanding. They laugh easily. They are easily grateful. They are never mean. They are not inhibited by fashion, public opinion or political correctness. They are exiles in their own communities, because they are always in a minority, but they form a mighty nation, if only they knew it.*'

 From Jan Morris's
 'Trieste and The Meaning of Nowhere'
France diary September 2001

So, what a sad last page for this trip. My last few days in Paris and nearing the end of a round world ticket with only carry-on luggage again. Now the paper tells of 24 suspected terrorists preparing to blow up 5 planes out of Heathrow. My flight delayed I'm told.

There they all were, all under 30 – Umir, Muhammed, Waheed, Assam and Assad, Osman, Abdul and of course young Brian Young, 28, of Wycombe, Buckinghamshire. Recently renamed himself as Umar Islam. A quiet lad and a nice boy according to his mother and neighbours. Of course, he's friggin' quiet! Is he really going to go and bang on at his local boozer about how he and his mates intend to substitute peroxide and nitro-glycerine for his baby shampoo and to bring down a 747?

Well, I'm completely over these fundamentalists, jihadists, Al-Qaeda operatives, Hezbollahists – call them what you like. Forcing me to now check-in my luggage. Making me stand and wait at baggage carousels. Preventing me carrying my champagne bottles on board in case the corks detonate in mid-flight.

Now I know young Brian, sorry Umar, sees the destroying or hijacking of a plane as having great symbolic values – after all the Boeing 747 was the last of the Great Machines that characterised the 20th century – it represents high technology and everything American and it made the world smaller.

Hijacking is now out of fashion and most seem to have ended with little or no loss of life. Negotiations took place, manuals were consulted and passengers went onto collect duty free at the end of the drama. But 9/11 changed all that.

Brian, there are six of you on the plane and 250 of us. We are not just going to sit there mate as we have nothing to lose, especially as I have had to most likely leave my bottles of champagne in Paris.

The vulnerability and beauty of that airliner cruising above the cloud line is always going to be there to tempt you, Brian, no matter what measures we introduce at airports to stop you.

But you will never, never win. Even if you have messed up my flight home tomorrow, I'm already planning the next flight. Brian, don't be on it. Or my next one after that.

Paris Journal
12 August 2006

And this part of the book really hit home, as I read the short story by Helen Garner,

'We heard he was back ... we wore what we thought was appropriate. We waited for him to declare himself, we waited for him to call.
No calls came. We discussed his possible whereabouts, the meaning of his silence, the possibilities of his future ...
His idea of this town is old. He's been away. He's lost the feel of it. He's been in Europe. He's been in America. He's been in the tropics. He's left. He's gone. He doesn't live here anymore. He's only visiting. He's only passing through ...'

    'The Dark, The Light'.

    Postcards from Surfers, (Penguin 2010)

Waikiki Beach

July 2007

Life is the same as it always was, unruffled by events, indifferent to the joys and sorrows of man, mute and incomprehensible as the Sphinx. But the stage on which the everlasting tragedy is enacted changes constantly to avoid monotony. The world we lived in yesterday is not the same world we live in today, inexorably it moves on through the infinite towards it's doom, and so do we. No man bathes twice in the same river, said Heraditus. Some of us crawl on our knees, some ride on horseback or in motor car; others fly past the carrier-pigeon in aeroplanes. There is no need for hurry, we are all sure to reach the journey's end.

    Axel Munthe,

    1930

The Flâneur is the consummate traveller and I've always aspired to this art form. But sadly he is becoming an endangered species, as individual travel is taken over by mass tourism, resort and cruise holidays, package tours etc.

As the writer Colin James observes, the flâneur was the sentient ambler through urban space. He – for the flâneuse was a rarity – was a characteristic figure of early 19th century culture.

The late French film critic André Bazin saw the flâneur as 'the sole true sovereign' of all of Paris, the individual immersed in the crowd but not of it, walking the streets of the city, experiencing the distinctive anonymity of the urban crowd and drinking in appearances.

Charles Baudelaire also summed it up nicely – 'for the perfect flâneur, for the passionate spectator, it is an immense joy to set up home in the heart of the multitude, amid the ebb and flow of movement, in the midst of the fugitive!'

Yes, the flâneur or flâneuse = a city dwelling idler who hovers at the periphery of crowds, browsing passers-by and buildings with the detached interest of a window shopper.

Paris journal 2016

Not exactly how I imagined 65 to be, but not too bad at all. Overlapping feelings of grief and elation.

Grief from losing two friends, Caroline from Wye and Derek from Melbourne. Grief from losing my business from the horrific bushfire in 2015, along with the associated friendships and clients built up over 25 years.

Elation from time out in Bali, Vietnam and France all in the last eight months.

And knowing that I never have to really work again, or at least when I really only want to, and to do only really what appeals.

And to keep travelling.

Paris - Saigon flight
August 2016

〰️
〰️

When a man has reached old age and has fulfilled his mission, he has a right to confront the idea of death in peace. He has no need of other men, he knows them already and has seen enough of them. What he needs is peace. It is not seemly to seek out such a man, plague him with chatter, and make him suffer banalities. One should pass by the door of his house as if no one lived there.

On the door of Henry Miller's house,

Los Angeles.

Lorne Foreshore, September 2017

... but you always end up where you're meant to be.

Acknowledgements

To all the books, publications and writings. To all the authors and writers who I've drawn inspiration from. To my wonderful publisher, Blaise. To Xavier and Latetia for the use each summer of their 'Tiger Cage' apartment in Paris. To Graham, Alan and Pat for reinstating my pulse. To you all, mille mercis.

Of course, any comments or spiteful throwaway remarks etc. designed or not to draw blood, will all be well received at martyjf@hotmail.com.

www.ingramcontent.com/pod-product-compliance
Lightning Source LLC
Chambersburg PA
CBHW021429080526
44588CB00009B/477